RUBY RED SHOES

EMPOWERING STORIES ON RELATIONSHIPS, INTUITION & PURPOSE

Compiled by: Kristine Gravelle-Rystenbil

Dear Janine,
I hope these stories
inspire you!
Chrissy Porter

LWL PUBLISHING HOUSE

Brampton, Canada

CONTENTS

The Freedom in Shedding My Layers
Angela T. Muskat

The Courage to Live Authentically
Tammy Roggie

The Value of a Scream
Sophia Zoe

Breaking Out and Finding Me
Oona Liz Nunez

LEGAL DISCLAIMER

The information and content contained within this book *Ruby Red Shoes – Empowering Stories on Relationships, Intuition & Purpose* does not substitute any form of professional counsel such as a Psychologist, Physician, Life Coach, or Counsellor. The contents and information provided does not constitute professional or legal advice in any way, shape or form.

Any decisions you make and the outcomes thereof are entirely your own do-ing. Under no circumstances can you hold the Author, LWL PUBLISHING HOUSE, or "Anita Sechesky – Living Without Limitations Inc." liable for any actions that you take.

You agree not to hold the Author, LWL PUBLISHING HOUSE, or "Anita Sechesky – Living Without Limitations Inc." liable for any loss or expense incurred by you, as a result of materials, advice, coaching or mentoring offered within.

The information offered in this book is intended to be general information with respect to general life issues. Information is offered in good faith; however you are under no obligation to use this information.

Nothing contained in this book shall be considered legal, financial, or actuarial advice.

The author assumes no liability or responsibility to actual events or stories be-ing portrayed.

It may introduce what a Life Coach, Counsellor or Therapist may discuss with you at any given time during scheduled sessions. The advice contained herein is not meant to replace the Professional roles of a physician or any of these professions.

FOREWORD

Every woman needs to know that she is cherished for exactly who she is. The foundation of *Ruby Red Shoes – Empowering Stories on Relationships, Intuition & Purpose*, was created from a beautiful vision that allowed the co-authors in this book to recognize that there's no fear in vulnerability when writing. By enabling their souls to be stirred, these writers are empowering so many multitudes of women throughout the world who need to feel heard, recognized as valuable, and appreciated for exactly who they are.

The stories that have come together to create this beautiful book are lovingly sewn together from the heart strings of each contributor. They are single, married, divorced, mothers, daughters, grandmothers, sisters, aunts, entrepreneurs, professionals, healers, and homemakers from all walks of life experiences. Some have never been published and took this opportunity to share something very personal with the whole, wide world. There are individuals who have called themselves writers, who have never stepped up to the plate like these women have. I am so proud and honored to be the publisher to each of these ladies. Their stories will cause you to examine your relationships in a new perspective, explore your intuition, and trust your feminine senses once again, as well as define what your true purpose in life really is.

So many people embark on personal journeys of self-discovery and healing, and never find the pathway to their destiny. An anthology is a work of art that brings the world to one place. Where else can you find thirty unique and gifted souls collaborating to empower one beautiful vision as they aspire *and* inspire, not only the people in their own lives, but thirty times over and so on. What initially impressed me about this amazing group is how they supported one another right from the start and have celebrated this journey all the way through to completion. This book is already a champion in women's books because the right people came together and honored the integrity of all women around the world.

Thank you Kristine and all the ladies of the Ruby Red Shoes Sisterhood. It has been a pleasure to work with you on this anthology and to be your publisher.

Anita Sechesky

Publisher, Registered Nurse, Certified Professional Coach, NLP and LOA Wealth Practitioner, Best-Seller Consultant, multiple International Best-Selling Author, Workshop Facilitator and Conference Host, Founder and CEO of Anita Sechesky - Living Without Limitations Inc. and the Founder and Publisher of LWL PUBLISHING HOUSE.

INTRODUCTION & VISION

Ruby Red Shoes: Empowering Stories of Relationship, Intuition and Purpose, is a vision that was two years in the making before it came to be this book.

My motivation for creating *Ruby Red Shoes* didn't come from a personal need to voice my own experience, get attention, or lead a group of women – the inspiration for this book was broader than that. It's been about being of service to bring a powerful vision for women into the world through the power of story on three themes that are common to and impact all women.

At its core, *Ruby Red Shoes* is a homecoming for women on a journey back to who they really are in the areas of relationship, intuition, and life purpose. Like Dorothy, as she makes her way through Oz, each woman in this book shares a personal Eureka and her life experience. She stands vulnerable and open before you as a leader and trailblazer in her own right, baring her soul in her own unique way.

Every woman has a special message waiting to be heard by those ready to hear it. In this book, you'll find ancient wisdom shared by soul sisters you haven't met. Some women have had a journey filled with illusions, nightmares, and challenges that are jaw-dropping – especially in cases where they experienced emotional trauma and lived to tell the tale. For other women, their journey's been more of a breeze.

No one said that the *Ruby Red Shoes* journey would be an easy one. In the school of life, many women experience a lot of hard knocks as they earn their racing stripes. What started off as a personal writing project for many of the women in this book, ended up being a Pandora's Box drawing out forgotten memories and uncovering buried emotions.

The stories in *Ruby Red Shoes*, call us to share ourselves authentically with others, to set realistic boundaries, and to ask for support. The women in this book use their life experiences to gently guide and inspire us on improving our self-esteem, having a healthy relationship with our self (and others), and trusting our inner voice.

Do you know what you were put on this Earth to do? Stories in this book cover that base too.

The common theme the women in this book share is that the most valuable resource you have in your life is YOU! They also remind us to use the power we have in our relationships, the power that comes with implicitly trusting our inner voice, and the power of self-actualization.

Any time we are exposed to heart-centred, inspiring, empowered, and purpose-driven women, we thrive, learn and blossom. Use the stories in *Ruby Red Shoes* to encourage and remind you that no matter where you are on your own Ruby Red Shoes journey, you are never alone, have a hand to hold, are infinitely powerful and have within, all of the answers that you seek.

I invite you to pour through the pages of *Ruby Red Shoes*, a book filled with empowering stories about the lives, hearts, and souls of women around the world. Thank you, my dear friends.

Love and big hugs!

Kristine

ACKNOWLEDGEMENTS

Here's where I remember the dear Angels who've shown up to guide, support, and nudge me in the direction I needed to go; without you, the landscape of my life and this project would look very different.

- My sweetie pie husband: You're my CFO, my daily reality check and soul partner. Sweetie, you rock!
- My children: You stretch me emotionally, remind me to laugh, and help me to remember the joy in childhood innocence.
- My father and dearly departed mother, sister Karen, and brother Michael: Through good times and bad, we continue to love one another.
- Annemarie, Connie, Evelyn, Gail, Giuliana, Heather, Irena, Luisa, Mary-Lynn, Monica and Nancy: You've traveled alongside me for many, many years through thick and thin. Thank you.
- Jodie, AlexSandra, the staff and my classmates from The Inner Focus School of Advanced Energy Healing: Thank you for helping me to remember my Higher Self, my direct connection with God, and for exposing me to mediation and a solid foundation of energy healing.
- Beth and Pamela: My gateway and mentors into the world of Scientific Hand Analysis. You helped me feel sane again. Thank you for guiding me on how to step into the power of my Moon Whorl, my gift markings, and the lines in my hand. As we know, the journey continues.
- Valentina, Gloria, Wilma, Douglas, Lori, Annie and the staff at Sheridan College: Thank you for being my creative cheerleaders.
- The GradUit, Melanie, Penny Lee, Liz, and Nicola: For introducing me to Dream Boards, business planning, supporting and encouraging me to keep moving forward each day (no matter what) with a step-by-step plan.
- Anita: Thank you for your support and for getting the ball rolling on this book by asking me the right questions.
- The women in the Ruby Red Shoes book project. For being courageous enough to step into this project; you've bared part of your soul in your own unique way. Thank you for your support and helping me step into the role of leader. I honor you.
- Wayne, Louise, Neal Donald, Doreen and James and Jennifer: For being the powerful Spiritual Teachers and Visionaries that you are.

- Rhonda, Ali, Lisa, Christian, Kendall, Callan and Justin, Steve: You inspire me with your expertise and business mindset.
- The kindred spirits who surround me daily: For helping me learn about the facets of my heart and my capacity to love.

DEDICATION

This Book is dedicated to all of the women in the world who are walking their own Ruby Red Shoes journey. I thank you from the bottom of my heart for your strength, perseverance, and wisdom; you inspire me.

Kristine Gravelle-Rystenbil

RELATIONSHIPS

How are the relationships in your life? Great, good, average, just plain awful? Ultimately, our goal is to seek out relationship with people that provides us with the encouragement, love, support and insight we need to grow more fully as women, so we can reach for the stars and emotionally excel in our life.

The most important relationship we can nurture and cultivate is the one we have with ourselves and our intuition. For most people, their relationship with self-love, self-value and self-esteem are weak at best. In fact, for many women it's only after they've experienced emotional bruising, physical violation, and the pain of loss are they motivated to begin the journey of claiming relationship mastery in their own lives.

Read on to find out how these **Ruby Red Shoes** women rose from the ashes to powerfully navigate the adventure of relationship in their own lives.

CHAPTER 1   ANGELA T. MUSKAT

The Freedom in Shedding My Layers

I have always wanted to tell my story; to write a book about the journey that has brought me to this point. Ironically, it is the actual process of writing my story down that has prevented me from sharing it – until now.

Life, for me, is about stripping away the layers that are not me; the me that is the core of who I am.

We become so many versions of ourselves in a lifetime. From the time we begin school and even before that, we adhere to "rules" that tell us how to behave, what to write on our exams, and what information is "relevant". We take on contextual ways of being the "good girl" at home, the one who always does the "right thing", the "good wife and mother", the "good employee", "the strong one" – and while our egos thrive, our souls wither.

I lost my father to suicide when I was eight-years-old and as a child I had no way of dealing with the pain, and the immense emotional turmoil surrounding his death. By the time I reached adulthood, not expressing my emotions had become normal for me. Creaking from the weight of many, many layers, my soul had withered to a point where I allowed cancer to grow in my body and the prognosis was bleak. I had two choices: either give up and give in, or prepare for the challenge of my life.

I didn't know that in challenging cancer, I would actually have to give up the "fight", release the victim I had allowed myself to become, and that I would find at the very core of this lesson, myself. The cancer became the gift that brought me to the core of who I *am*, and allowed me to release the layers of who I thought I *had* to be.

My journey has been one of stripping away the layers and much of what doesn't serve me at my core. I shared with friends that since I devoted myself to inner healing, I don't wear earrings anymore, because I feel they interfere with my energy. Jewelry, makeup, even the wrong outfit interferes with the energy I feel and have to share.

When I strip away the outer trappings of life related to how I look, or how I *should* feel, I am left with my essential self. Now I only layer on what feels natural to me and my body, like essential oils; a key component in healing myself at a cellular level.

I am paying more attention to what *is* and *isn't* Ego, and do checks to assess my attachment; I continually ask myself, "Do I really love and need this in my life? Is it serving an ego purpose, or is my very being served by it?"

Horses are close companions of mine; six of them live with me. Even though, I could never imagine my life without them, at one point I assessed their presence in my life. I stepped away from them, focusing only on the basics: Keep them clean, fed, and healthy. I didn't spend any extra time with them.

I had no expectations that they would "love me back," nor were they responsible for my happiness in any way. I was amazed that when I allowed myself to be vulnerable and detached, these amazing creatures actually grew closer to me.

Author Linda Kohanov states, *"The equine system is like a huge receiver and amplifier for emotional vibrations. No matter how good you are at hiding things from yourself and others, your nervous system still involuntarily broadcasts what you're really feeling, at a frequency horses are especially good at tuning into."*

What I found was, when I am not true to myself and covered by layers of unacknowledged judgement, my horses don't trust me; it's almost like I'm pushing them away. When I'm my true vulnerable self, they accept me and embrace me into the herd.

One of the most valuable lessons I have struggled with was in my marriage. I learned in a very painful way that I can't change my life in trying to control other people and outer circumstances. The only way to make life changes is stripping off my own layers of accumulated hurts and pains, staggered on through false beliefs about myself and the world around me.

My husband and I were married for twenty years. I still remember the first time I saw him in a crowded community center; even though we were children, it felt like I found an old friend. He and I parented two beautiful sons and now enjoy spending time with our grandchildren. Although we are divorced, we truly love each other. This is a bond that has defied time, space and circumstance, but had to be recovered under many layers.

In 2003, when I was forty-years-old, we emigrated from Germany to Ontario, Canada. We purchased a beautiful property in the Ottawa Valley and had plans of turning it into a guest retreat. Within two years of arriving, a huge tumor started to grow inside of me and a rare form of cancer was diagnosed.

Looking back, I can see, how moving to a new country and being without a network of close family and friends, would bring up fears, unhealed and unresolved issues, and insecurities that I didn't even know existed, but finally came to great me rather forcefully.

Years of not paying attention to my feelings from childhood on, and allowing unexpressed anger and resentment to settle in the deepest parts of my being, provided a perfect fertile breeding ground for the cancer to grow. Suddenly, I had to look at myself, how I rejected myself and how I had been living my life rather unconsciously.

The process of working through the cancer and the buried memories and pain that manifested it, have taken years of deep inner healing work. I changed my entire life; from the way I think, eat, breathe, work, and exercise, to who I allow in my life.

I believe that all of life is energy, and I have learned to be discerning about how and with whom I share this energy. Life is precious; the cancer really taught me that. I am precious, and I am worthy of my own love. I am here for a reason. Taking responsibility for my life and living and gaining more awareness is a big part of it.

People speak of having to *"beat"* and *"fight"* cancer. I learned to embrace the cancer and to love it, so that I can be at peace with it. At peace with the cancer, myself, and all my accumulated layers; that was the first step into stripping them off and letting them go.

I believe that dis-ease is a state of not being at ease with ourselves and the larger world; it is somehow connected to a fear of being seen in the world in all of our brilliance.

Marianne Williamson writes in her book, "Our deepest fear is not that we are inadequate. Our deepest fear is that we are powerful beyond measure. It is our Light, not our Darkness, that most frightens us."

I was not aware that there was a part of me that was frightened of life till recently. Actually, writing my story has brought that to my attention and gave me the opportunity to shed another layer. I've wanted to share this for years, but blocked myself because I judged myself as a terrible writer. I also didn't want to be seen. I've needed to ask clients and friends how I present myself, because some part of me has not been able to see and embrace my brilliance. It was time; time to follow the call and step into the brilliance and the love and the light that I am.

The more I am learning to accept my light, others around me are changing and the world outside of me is transforming. Universal Law states that a healed self is a healed world.

Looking back and recognizing all the layers I shed; if given the choice between cancer *or* living my life unconsciously, buried under those layers of false beliefs and repressed emotions, I'd choose the cancer. I love where I am at and who I am *now.*

Although the journey hasn't ended yet, I keep discovering and shedding layers. My raw, vulnerable, open-hearted and authentic self longs to shine and is needed to keep transforming my world.

It was cancer that woke me up to this, but there are other life challenges that can come to call. Our journeys are all different, but the same in many ways. I found my message of healing and love in the chaos and the pain. My layers, once removed, revealed that.

Angela T. Muskat immigrated to Canada from Germany in 2003. She is a mother to two adult sons and an "Oma" to three Grandchildren. Angela studied in Industrial Business and Bank Management Administration. Primarily educated by life itself and hit by the cosmic 2x4 more than once, Angela is passionate about supporting people to take charge of their own lives so they can find their personal power.

Angela is a certified and trained Reiki Master/Teacher for humans and animals, Access Bars Facilitator, and Reflexologist. She uses these modalities to reach out to people and give them the right tools to work with.

Website: www.angelamuskat.com

Facebook: Angela T. Muskat - Love Life - Energy Connections

CHAPTER 2   TAMMY ROGGIE

The Courage to Live Authentically

One of my saddest memories is the day my sons' father left our marital home, leaving behind him broken hearts and dreams, and one small boy crying at the window, begging his father to take him with him.

Almost twenty years later that memory still brings tears to my eyes. How is it that we can hurt so much, yet find the will to go on?

Author Mark Nepo writes about how we are required by life to endure and endear when life is painful; that this is the place where tremendous growth often takes place.

How did I find the courage to endure and endear myself to the life I had created? I was raising my children alone in a city hundreds of miles from my family, and I often felt unanchored by a lack of connection. However, I chose to stay in that city as a single parent and began studies towards a Masters Degree in Pastoral Care and Counseling. It was God's grace and love that carried us every day; I saw it clearly in the kindness and support of family, friends, and strangers. There was a very real knowledge that we were not alone.

Looking back, it has been grace, love, forgiveness, and the healing power of time and circumstance that have allowed me and my sons' father to be close friends and allies. It took him a year and a half to realize that living so far away from his children was destroying him on a heart and soul level, and hurting our children. He moved back to the city where we lived, and we began the task of co-parenting in separate homes.

In that time, I remarried. To anyone who has created a stepfamily, it is not for cowards. As two families coming together to create something new, I can honestly say that we didn't always handle it well. There was incredible stress and what I can see now were power struggles. We made a mess of things; undeniably. We acted out of our own needs and insecurities and it was rough. Those years of animosity and unnecessary stress took their toll on our children as the adults in their lives were not doing well. Again, time is the healer. I have found forgiveness for myself and all of the parents involved. Our children have grown into fine young men.

As the years passed, things got easier. In their early teens, our sons used to remark that their father and I should give advice to divorcing parents on how to healthfully raise their children. They felt we had done a wonderful job of co-parenting, and should share what we had learned. We laughed, knowing that the journey to that healing and maturity took effort, love, and vision beyond ourselves.

My sons' dad and I sometimes attend the same social functions, and people still comment about our peaceful energy and ease with each other. They joke about how easy divorce seems and wonder why they haven't tried it! To them it seems that we have something miraculous and simple. We just laugh and remain grateful that we have managed to endure and endear ourselves to this life we have created.

This past Christmas reminded me of the many situations we have graciously navigated since our separation at the end of 1997. Seated at the brunch table was my current partner, my ex-husband and his partner, and our two sons. The conversation flowed, and I felt deeply loved by the five beautiful men who graced my table. I could not have foreseen that almost twenty years ago when my son stood at the window and cried for a father who was leaving home.

Time is a great healer, isn't it? I love the saying that we can allow it to make us bitter or better. I have never felt bitter about divorcing my sons' father. He is gay; a truth that wasn't revealed until years after our divorce. When that fact became known I felt like Atlas at the moment he shrugged; the weight of the world was suddenly taken off my shoulders. For years, I harbored the idea that I was a terrible wife and mother, and that is why he could not love me. It was neither of those things, he assured me. He just couldn't live a lie any longer.

It was a revelation of buried truths when he came forward with his news. I remembered many signs that pointed to his homosexuality, most especially how our lives changed when we came back from our honeymoon and he suddenly became very moody and angry and impatient with me and his life.

I began to shut down because his unhappiness was like an infection. I didn't know how to separate myself from his heavy and quickly changing moods. At first, I focused on my pregnancy, which in itself was miraculous as we were told we would never have children. Being told we were pregnant was a wonderful shock, because months would pass and he wouldn't touch me. Eventually it became years between any kinds of physical affection.

When you see photos of me from that time, I look vacant and neglected. I was on auto-pilot and completely immersed in loving and raising my children, and living like a roommate with their father. It was brutally hard.

I am a passionate, loving woman who needs affection. I grew up in household where my parents touched each other a lot, and other people would comment on their love and commitment to each other. I knew when I grew up I wanted that same kind of relationship filled with physical affection and closeness.

What I experienced was foreign to me. After almost seven years of this pain and anguish I asked for a separation. He was angry with me, but I knew I couldn't continue living that way. It was also a gift, as it turned out, because it forced him to confront his own truths and embrace them, and it propelled me into other relationships that really helped me learn about myself and forced me to take care of my needs.

I am waking more and more to the importance that I must give myself. Our children are now adults and no longer living at home. There is only myself to consider, and that is proving interesting. Suddenly, I have to learn to love who I am, with my equal amounts of perfection and scars. It is not easy to have to face and accept yourself when the roles you have been playing for years are stripped away.

I no longer identify as the mother and the ex-wife. "Who am I, really?" is a big question I am trying to answer. Once again I am called to endure and endear as life changes and evolves into new ways of being. I now see enduring and endearing as causes for celebration. I am finding and celebrating new ways of being in the world that are equally valid and becoming more comfortable.

As for my children's father and I, we both recently celebrated our 50th birthdays. We attended each other's celebration. At each event we embraced and shared the words, "I love you." We do love each other. We have created beautiful life together, and memories that we will never share with anyone else. We both know what it's like to yearn for those days when our boys were small and adored us and counted on us for their very survival. But we have also learned that there is something wonderful we have created beyond our family, and that is an enduring love that defies divorce.

We have matured and honored our humanity and the soul in each other, and are truly grateful for the gift of our children. He's a fine father, and I am a wonderful mother. Beyond those roles we know that the gift of simply thanking one another for being authentic and having shared some important moments in time has made life even more worthwhile. We are enduring friends. That is something to celebrate and endear us to life.

Tammy Roggie is a Spiritual Teacher, Healer, Connector, and student of life. She is also an elementary teacher in Cambridge, Ontario. She holds a Master's Degree in Counseling, is a dynamic inspirational speaker, a Yoga Instructor, Reiki Practitioner, Author and abstract painter.

Tammy likes to travel and collect stories from the people she meets. She is deeply interested in the power of story as a healing tool. Tammy's own journey continues to take her on interesting paths connected to the heart and soul of life. She can be reached through Facebook, or through her blog.

Facebook: Tammy Roggie

Blog: www.sisterhoodjunction.wordpress.com

CHAPTER 3   SOPHIA ZOE

The Value of a Scream

I loved working from home. I loved my apartment, with its two-story layout and huge windows. After years of personal turmoil, I was on track. Thirty-three years old and single. Twenty-eight fantastic piano students coming to my apartment for lessons. Amazing energy healing clients coming to see me for regular sessions.

New neighbors became increasingly problematic. Violent alcoholic rages, cursing, smashing things. We shared a wall that looked like standard drywall, but had the soundproofing capacity of tissue paper. To wit: "Where are you, grandma?" "I'm going poo."

The father next door stepped up his drinking, becoming verbally abusive to his wife and kids. The wife became physically abusive; almost daily, I heard "Don't hurt my daddy!"

Trickle effect? I lost my income. The parents of my piano students were appalled at the language they heard through the walls. They politely said "We're taking a break from piano lessons." My adult students were blunt: "Everything I'm hearing reminds me of my childhood. Coming here is too painful. Let me know if they move."

Since my healing room shared a wall with the neighbors, anyone in it incurred greater trauma. I had to refuse my healing clients. Within three weeks, I lost all of my income.

My landlord had a strange prejudice against me "A single woman should not have such a large apartment. You have too many books. Stop telling lies and bothering the nice family!" I wished the lady next door would throw things at him, too.

I called the police to get protection for the children – a girl, two, and a boy, eleven. I even feared for my own safety many times. Police responded to my 9-1-1 phone calls, but they frustrated and confused me. I felt like I was being interrogated. I told a friend about their bizarre behavior – always questioning me in accusing tones.

My friend, who had worked in family mediation, had much experience with the police. She looked at me like I was an idiot and said "It sounds to me like you think the police are your friends. They are not your friends. They have one job – to find holes in your story. Avoid speaking to them."

Wow. Eye-opening, paradigm-shifting news. This from an intelligent, law-abiding, kind-hearted woman. I had to believe her, get over my stunned state, and find a job to keep body and soul together.

When I hit crisis level, a friend rescued me with a job at her company. Not my dream job. I spent from 5:00 pm to 11:00 pm calling car owners across Canada, offering to book their oil changes. I took a train and a bus to get to a shady part of town. Getting home after midnight was frightening – twice I was followed most of the way home. I feared an assault. Being on high alert at 1:00 am drains the immune system.

A temporary agency placed me with a satellite TV service. They paid two dollars more per hour than the first job. I was to answer customer inquiries and take payments, etc. Simple stuff. Except, before training was over, a manager walked into our room of thirty new hires and said "This class will now be trained as technical support."

I wanted to run away. Tech support?! Nooo! I despise technical details. But I was stuck. The neighbors hadn't moved. They were still throwing things at each other that I expected would crash through the thin wall at any moment and strike me in the skull. My degrees in Music and Drama were weeping in their frames. I was now tech support for satellite TV, which I didn't even have.

After training, my class was assigned the worst shift: 3:30 pm to midnight, Wednesday to Sunday. I would get home around 1:30 am, unwind for two hours and go to bed around 3:30 am.

Psycho-spiritually, I began to fade. With those work days and hours, I couldn't see any friends or family. My body's natural rhythm went way off, I was bloated and grumpy, had weird aches and pains, and dragged myself around. I became depressed, hated my job, my neighbors, my landlord, and my life.

One night at work, I had excruciating menstrual cramps. Bent over at my computer in pain, I took a call from a Vietnamese grandmother who spoke to me in broken English. When I offered to get her a Vietnamese representative, she sounded offended and said, "No. Me English good. You help now."

And we began. I understood that she had no picture when she turned on the TV. I followed the trouble-shooting protocol – painstaking enough with native English speakers, never mind with syntax-inverting speakers.

My cramps felt like swords being thrust into my lower abdomen. I could hardly breathe as I tried to maintain a cheerful, customer-servicey tone. I managed to get the woman to understand that she needed to "put the phone down, go to the receiver...the black box under the TV...and unplug it from the wall for two minutes." The sound of her putting her telephone on a table was very clear. I heard her footsteps fading. Suddenly, a sharp pain hit me and I muttered "Oh my God, I can't take this anymore." Two minutes later, I heard footsteps and the garbled sound of the customer picking up the telephone. We proceeded, and she got her picture back. I went to a clinic the next day and found out I had a bladder infection in addition to having menstrual cramps. No wonder the pain was unbearable!

On my next shift, my supervisor called me in to discuss my first evaluation. He had randomly selected a call to evaluate - my call with the Vietnamese grandmother!

I did well, until the comment I'd made when the pain hit. That comment fell into a communications category that was heavily weighted. Thinking I was talking about the customer, my supervisor said "You're lucky the customer didn't hear you."

I pointed out the sound of the phone, her footsteps, her coming back...she obviously had not been on the phone when I said "Oh my God..."

He maintained his stance, and I received a big, fat ZERO in that category. Because of the evaluation's weighting, my final score was 32%. I was polite, friendly, efficient, and competent. His evaluation was ludicrous. I actually let out a little laugh. Mr. Supervisor put down his pen, faced me squarely and said "Based on this evaluation, YOU ARE NOT A VALUED EMPLOYEE."

I shot out of body. I looked down at us. This guy, half my height, ten years my junior, who was a DJ on weekends, just told me *I wasn't valued* – at a job I hated, but needed to take and work five times as many hours to make the same income I used to make at home – which wasn't even possible. And my I.Q. was 100 points too high for this stupid call centre job. How dare an employer tell anyone they aren't valued! That should be illegal. He said he'd give me another chance, because he was a *nice* guy.

Standing on the subway platform that night, waiting for the last train, I understood why people commit suicide. After so many struggles, disappointment, humiliation, and unhappy twists, being alienated from everyone and not feeling safe at home – why live?

I heard the subway train approaching the station. A distraught voice in my head said, "*Jump!*" Instead, I screamed. Loud. From the bottom of my torso. The train swooshed in, brakes screeching, wind flapping unbuttoned coats and flinging hair around.

I froze. Had anyone heard me? I looked to my right. The woman was not staring at me. I looked to my left. That man had not noticed me. No one had heard me scream. The tightness in my chest was gone. I felt like I'd discovered a marvelous secret: *Covert Public Screaming for Stress Relief.* I did it every night from then on. It was amazingly therapeutic.

The next week, another evaluation. My score was 98%. The supervisor congratulated me on my fast and vast improvement. I told him I had not improved; all my calls were good. He blinked and repeated himself. I endured five months there. When I told my supervisor I had found a new job, he tried to get me to stay. No way, DJ! Like the wrongfully accused being released from prison, I rushed out of the building and danced down the steps. I was free!

I am so grateful that on that fateful night my mind was overruled by my body's impulsive solution: to scream. Screaming was perfect. It took five seconds to release the stress and defeat I experienced daily. I am glad that no one heard me that day, otherwise, I might have been considered crazy. All the words I couldn't safely express came out all at once, in one big guttural sound. Screaming kept me sane. Screaming kept me alive.

Sophia Zoe is a Holistic Practitioner who uses many forms of alternative and complementary healing techniques for stress and trauma relief. A passion for the natural and alternative saw a fifteen-year-old Sophia begin her journey as a healer. Decades later, what began as self-education led to a rewarding career helping people.

Sophia's training in theatre, voiceovers, film, and television make her an enjoyable media guest. She has appeared on local talk shows, radio shows, and on international web TV. Sophia gained much popularity on global telesummits, doing live group healings.

Website: www.SophiaZoe.com

Facebook: Sophia Zoe - Energy Fix

CHAPTER 4   OONA LIZ NUNEZ

Breaking Out and Finding Me

Today, I sit in front of my computer wondering what I should share with you. I've been on this earth for thirty-seven years, yet I've experienced more in those years than most people I know.

Civil wars, sexual assault, rape, bullying, moving to a new city and a new country, learning a new culture, and new languages, adapting to a new life style, getting married, being a mother to four kids, accidents, surgeries, a brain tumor...the list goes on. I don't know if my life is exciting, but what I do know is that there's certainly never a dull moment.

I was born in a third world country, within a cast system. Although this was never discussed everyone knew where their place in society was, and if they didn't, there was someone that would "kindly" remind them.

From an early age, I was taught that I should be a certain way and follow a certain path. I was too shy and scared to argue. I was the "good girl", the "obedient one". My teachers praised me and my aunts and uncles saw me as a role model.

At school, I was bullied, pushed aside, and ostracized by my classmates. With family, if adults were present, my cousins (who despised me) would pretend to play with me, but when the adults turned their backs, they'd avoid me and treated me like an outcast.

As a young child, I didn't understand why others were so mean, hurtful, and cruel. I was too young to understand why people, especially those my age, didn't like me. I was quiet, shy, and I didn't like conflict, yet conflict found me everywhere I went.

While situations like this would cause most people to hide and learn to blend in with the walls and furniture, I actually found them interesting and fun. I would sit still for hours and watch the people around me, studying their mannerisms, their faces, and attitudes. I turned my study into a private game to see if I could guess what people would do next based on what I'd observed.

Even though I was treated poorly by people, I had an amazing childhood filled with love, adventure, and imagination. I have two wonderful, loving, and amazing parents who love each other and cherish me and my siblings. I have two fantastic siblings whom I'm close to and adore.

Growing up was a learning experience. My family was fortunate enough to be considered "upper class". We had maids, a chauffeur, and a beautiful house. But my mother would never let this get to our heads. I remember how she would get down on her hands and knees to show the girls who worked for us how to care for the floor. She would spend hours in the kitchen showing them how to cook and prepare our meals. She has never been afraid to get her well-manicured hands dirty.

My mother has always said, "There is no shame in the type of work you do, or where you come from. What makes a person who they are is their dedication, their effort, and their integrity. What's important is who you choose to be, and the difference you make in other people's lives." I have always lived by this mindset.

When I was growing up, I never really confided in anyone, nor did I tell anyone how others had treated me. Even after I'd been sexually assaulted (at the age of four), I kept quiet. There were times when I would hurt and feel sad, but then there were other times, when out of the blue, I would meet a kindred soul and my world would light up.

I was twelve when we moved to a new country. It was an exciting yet frightening time. Other than a couple of people, my family knew no one and we didn't speak the language; however, I was a motivated teenager. I wanted to learn French in order to understand what people were saying, and watching my favorite TV shows was how I did it. Yes, I admit it – I was a TV-aholic.

In my teens, I was shy and awkward. Because we immigrated to Canada in November, the school year was two months underway. I was petrified of being singled out and wanted to hide my head in the sand like an ostrich. I knew no one, hardly spoke French or English and no one spoke Spanish either.

Despite of my fears, something life-changing happened when I started school – I was put into a class of ten kids, none of whom spoke French. All of the kids in my class were from different countries, with different views and cultures. We didn't speak the language and we all craved acceptance; we bonded instantly. For the first time in my life, I felt like I belonged – I felt normal. It was exciting and fascinating. As time passed, more kids came into the class. Our small group grew and with it so did friendships that would stand the test of time.

Being in this class with this group changed my mindset and my view of the world. I no longer felt like my life was predetermined, and new opportunities started showing up. By the end of my first year in that class, I felt different. I was learning new things about myself and how I interacted with others; I realized that people were not scary, they were just human.

As time passed, I still felt shy and awkward approaching and talking with people; I was afraid of being rejected and embarrassed.

I remember one day at school, I was sitting on the floor, in front of my locker doing one of my favorite things – people watching. I remember seeing a girl walk up to a group of popular kids and start talking with them. I was shocked and baffled! How could a seemingly *regular* girl walk up and talk to the cool kids? *(In high school the popular crowd were like Gods; everyone wanted to be like them, be friends with them, and be known by them)*. As I sat there watching them interact with her, it suddenly dawned upon me that if she could do it, so could I!

Armed with my new found knowledge, I stood up and went to talk to the popular kids! To my amazement, they were just like everyone else. They were funny, caring, and they actually knew who I was! I was amazed. From that point on, I wasn't afraid to talk to other people, and I found it fun.

My College and University years flew by. I was more confident, but innocent and very naïve. I believed that everyone was nice and that they had no hidden agenda. Sadly, I was wrong; there are some people in the world who are not kind.

For many years, I'd done a lot of soul searching and followed Mother Teresa's teachings. I was twenty-one when I decided to become a nun. I'd made my appointment on a Thursday with a Mother Superior to join her convent, excited to be following in the amazing footsteps of my role model.

But that weekend everything changed, and my world was turned upside down after someone raped me.

Because I lost my virginity in that situation, I no longer felt worthy. I felt dirty, ashamed, and embarrassed. And I withdrew my application from the convent.

When I finally told someone what had happened, those around me made me feel as if it was my fault, like I'd asked for it, and that I had put myself in that situation.

Shocked, horrified, and insulted, I didn't know what to say, or how to respond.

And that's when something in me snapped. An anger so deep and powerful roared inside of me, coursing through my veins, my body, and soul. The sleeping beast that had lain dormant for so many years was awake AND it was done taking crap from anyone.

That day was a turning point in my life. I refused to be a victim – I was a survivor. After all I'd been through, I'd made it this far and I would keep on going! I decided not to be a nun and hide behind a robe to help others. I was me, and I was choosing to live life and help those that wanted my help.

Many more things have since happen in my life, but I've learned to *know me*, to *listen to me* and to really *be me*. I have been to hell and back many times, and each time I come out stronger, wiser, and happier.

Oona Liz Nunez is a Blogger, Motivational Speaker, Therapeutic Touch Practitioner, proud wife and mother to three children. Oona graduated from Concordia University with a degree in Translation. She also volunteered and worked as an intervener for a Sexual Assault Centre.

In mid-2014, Oona was diagnosed with a Brain Tumor which was partially removed via surgery later that year. Although her recovery is ongoing and quite challenging, she is a beacon of sunshine and positivity to people around her and to new people she meets.

Facebook : Oona Liz

Blog: https://oonaliz.wordpress.com/

CHAPTER 5   JACQUELINE RICHARDS

How Missing a Train Improved My Relationship with My Daughter

In the single parent realm, I have always found it interesting how my daughter knew exactly which gifts were from mommy and which ones were from daddy, and that events often carried a price tag and what the amount was. She knew the difference between one dollar versus ten dollars and what an amount beyond one hundred dollars meant when it came to having extraordinary life adventures.

At the same time, my daughter knows about gifts and their value. She hasn't fully grasped how her mommy's space-time continuum works. The space-time continuum is a mathematical model that joins space and time into a single idea. Had my daughter fully understood how this theory is something I play with in day-to-day life, she might have decided to miss the train to a priceless life journey.

A question about adventures: Isn't the journey supposed to be about the experiences and love exchanged in play – not the dollar value? For example, heading to a provincial park to play badminton and enjoy peanut butter and jelly sandwiches. Or what about the fun of giggling and jumping in warm rain puddles beneath the rainbow, after watching and listening to a loud thunderstorm? These are loving and priceless experiences.

My little girl is graduating from grade six in a month, and I have a sense that she will expect more than parks and puddles for this occasion; especially since her daddy adventures had me competing with a five day cruise and then with Disneyland. Celebrating her graduation is my chance to inherit the title of outstanding mommy.

In fine mommy form, I decide to raise the bar by arranging an extraordinary *Educational Vacation*. I tripped on information about Percé, Quebec. For us, this unexplored and beautiful location is a perfect adventure. I will book two rooms at a waterfront Bed and Breakfast, then I, the unilingual mommy, will watch my baby girl practice both official languages as we whale watch. We will eat fine foods and hike in great spaces. I will rent kayaks so we can travel on the St. Lawrence River and visit Percé Rock.

Yahoo. Mommy is taking flight on this best Parent game.

As a mortgage agent and entrepreneur, networking builds my business. One evening, I attended a fundraising event with great business women, guest speakers, and a silent auction. The angels were on my side – one of the auction items was two VIA rail tickets for anywhere in Canada. I didn't need anywhere; I only needed Percé, Quebec!

The bidding began at a better than fair price. I bid in increments of $10.00. A competitor bid in $1.00 increments. I had an issue when the Silent Auction bidding ended after a $1.00 bid and no tickets for me. Once the intrigue settled, I phoned around and purchased two Economy Train Tickets at the final bidding price. I upgraded to a private room with two beds and assured my husband, that mom-daughter weekend was worth it.

Knowing my best friend and her daughter would also love this kind of escape, I called her and the first comment was, "Is this a safe adventure, Jacqueline?"

"What did she mean by that?" I thought. Then she commented, "Sure. Sounds like fun and we are traveling without cell phones and computers!"

This is perfect! I'll keep our accommodations at the waterfront Bed and Breakfast my secret. The amazing book that I had ordered arrives in time for our Percé adventure. My mom-daughter surprise is coming together.

Departure day arrives. I have 'lots to get done before I go – a workaholic always does. Focus, Jacqueline. I made sure my daughter is packed for the trip. I am not, but it won't take long for me to complete that task. We need to leave the house at 4 p.m. to make the train.

My husband walks into my home office suggesting that I pack up now so we arrive at the train station on time. He's helpful when he's not interrupting me.

Again, "Jacqueline, I think it's time to go. It's 3pm."

Again, "Jacqueline it's 3:15."

After the fourth interruption, "Jacqueline it is 3:30."

The conversation gets intense. I tell my husband that leaving at 4 p.m. gets us to the train on time. He hands me the train tickets to confirm the train's departure time.

"Arrive by 3:30 P.M for 4 P.M. DEPARTURE". What?! OMG!

My daughter is waiting at the door with her favourite blanket. My husband pulls the car up to the front door and opens the truck for baggage. I close my office, shut down my cell phone and computer, then bound up the stairs to pack a tote bag and the new book. I nearly trip down the stairs on my way to the front door. My daughter is staring at Mom in wonderment.

"Her time-space!" My husband is thinking as he races to the door screaming, "Jacqueline! Get in the car!" His wife has done it again.

At 3:50 pm...in traffic...from west to east...without traffic lights or slow drivers...I might be late by twenty minutes. Today, every delay possible happens.

Yes, I missed the train, but I will not be defeated. I ask my husband, "The next train station's only two hours away. Will you drive us to Montreal?" I hear his call of the wild. "Jacqueline! Get in the car!"

An hour into the drive we meet with limited traffic. I proposed that we increase our speed after seeing flashing lights behind us. The lights belong to an unmarked police car and are meant especially for us. With my daughter sitting in the back seat, screaming a bad "F" word is not an option.

A calm, cool, and collected police officer took identification and insurance. She asked why we were speeding with kids in the car. "We are trying to get to the train station. On time," my husband calmly replied. Slowly, he took the $200.00 ticket - losing zero demerit points. Phew! Continuing, we weren't driving nearly as quickly.

Montreal is a beautiful city and the downtown core has many one way streets. Calm, cool, and collected is not our Montreal mantra at this point in time. The train station is a heritage building located on a two way street. We pull in. I hear the sound of a horn and the gears of a train – leaving!

I roll out of the car. This is not possible! One might call me unlucky. I think it's a time-space continuum issue. Parked illegally, I wonder what the next move is. Planes, trains and automobiles are out. Where is the bus station?

At 9 p.m., I bought both of them dinner. I needed to thank my husband for his loving tolerance, and my little girl who is very unsure about the situation.

We are leaving on the midnight bus to Percé, Quebec. It's a twenty hour ride that includes a stop in Rimouski. Picking up on the *Education Vacation* theme, Rimouski has historic landmarks and it's a pit stop fifteen hours into our journey.

Boarding the bus is an older gentleman who takes a seat in front of us. I need to confess to my daughter, "Sweetie, I'm so sorry for putting you through this. I just wanted to celebrate your graduation." She pulls me close and says, "I love you Mommy. I'm happy just to be with you." A hug and then she whispers, "I smell pee. I think it's the man in front of us."

We read the first three chapters of the new book and eat the two chocolate bars I bought at the bus station.

The bus door opens at the sign that says LAND'S END (GASPÉ - PERCÉ) near the tip of the Gaspé Peninsula. We're gleefully skipping, because there's only one way to get to the Bed and Breakfast.

When we arrive, the General Manager says, "Bonjour .You must be Jacqueline Richards. Your friend, is she with you?" OH NO!! She doesn't know where we are staying and she has no cell phone!

I call my friend's mother who confirms that she arrived in Percé, but "After waiting twenty hours for you, they got back on the train and are heading home."

Hearing the conversation, the General Manager asks if she can help. "Yes please." I say. She calls the VIA train conductor and asks him to find my friend.

"Here's the phone, Jacqueline" and she hands me the receiver. I can't believe the conductor found her! My first words to her, "I'm in Percé and I'm so sorry! Please get off the train! I'm sending a taxi for you."

A short while later, my friend and her daughter re-arrive with sun hats and tote bags in hand and I get the "Seriously, Jacqueline!" gaze. Then, instinctively we laugh, hug, and begin the Percé adventure. It was an awesome trip.

Returning home, (by train this time) it occurred to me that even the best laid plans can go very south when trying to go northeast. In creating exciting experiences with positive outcomes the race to the tickets...the train station...the bus...the best friend...all were impacted by my decision to be the best mom ever. I need to take a breath

Plans with kids, no matter how they go, kids appreciate what you've offered – no matter how off-script it may be. Children are more forgiving when parents own their boo-boos. Friends who witness your bedlam will forgive too.

As my Yoga Gurus have written, we only have so many breaths. So, breathe deeply and lean into a calm mind space and move forward to allow the path to appear.

And so it shall be. I will continue planning and sharing charming journeys on my personal space-time continuum.

My new F-word is, FAN-FREAKIN'TASTIC. It was the best trip ever!

"To wish you were someone else is to waste the person you are." ~ Sven Goran Eriksson

As an Accredited Mortgage Professional, Jacqueline Richards finds clients effective mortgages and borrowing strategies. First-time home buyers, single parent families, and real estate investors find her mortgage-related seminars are instrumental in decision-making.

Jacqueline authored *Yoga For Your Personal Finances* based on practical solutions to health, wealth, and spirit blending postures and wealth solutions key to enriching physical well-being, personal wealth, and goals.

A proud participant on the Prime Minister's Task Force on Female Entrepreneurs, Jacqueline is a past Co-Chair of Canadian Women in Communication (NCR) and Ottawa Chamber of Commerce Board Director. Jacqueline is a Yoga Teacher and International Speaker.

Website: www.wealthy-yogini.com

Facebook: YogaForYourPersonalFinances

CHAPTER 6   JOANNE ALLAIRE

Letting Go, To Grow

From the age of five until my early teens, I was intimately violated by a close family member. I struggled for years to keep my secret hidden, thinking that I could *deal with the situation* myself.

I succeeded in living a quasi-normal life 'til the age of twelve, when one of my aunts - who'd experienced the same thing as a child – saw through my charade and took me aside privately to find out what was going on. As I spilled my heart and soul out to her, she comforted me. When I was done, she lovingly said, "It's time to let people know. I'll support you."

Bit-by-bit, I began to reveal to my family what had been happening; however, with the perpetrator still in my life (but no longer violating me), sharing my truth was very challenging. My heart longed to receive a sincere apology for all of the hurt that I'd been subjected to. At the time, I was angry. I wanted the individual to admit they'd made a mistake and give me the respect that I'd been denied! Instead, they brushed the situation off, like dirt under the corner of a carpet.

Between the ages of thirteen and eighteen, my life was a roller coaster full of adventure and experiences. I refer to this time as my *Personal Dark Ages,* because it was a time where I denied my true self and walled off my emotions.

During my personal *Dark Ages,* I was on automatic pilot and behaved in ways that reinforced my feelings of low self-esteem and worthlessness.

- I lead the life of a social butterfly, surrounding myself with people whom I called *friends*, but keeping the *real* me and my feelings locked behind walls and thick barriers.
- I also made a point of not going to social and family gatherings. Holidays like Thanksgiving, Christmas and Easter were marketing traps

and relationship cobwebs that were to be avoided at all costs; if I could escape from celebrating them, I was a happy camper.

- I tried desperately to get approval of everyone in school, at work, and in my private life.

As my *Dark Ages* came to an end, I sought out therapy to heal my heart, mind, and life. Surprisingly, it was outside my therapy sessions that I made the most progress in rebuilding my self-esteem.

* * *

My god-mother (my aunt) had a favorite saying, "You can overcome anything if you put your mind to it." I loved this motto, so much so that I adopted it; however, it was only years later (after my aunt's passing), did I realize how fundamental a part of my mindset her words had become in helping me release my past, boost my self-esteem, and determine the kind of legacy I want to leave behind when I die.

In addition to that mantra, my aunt also gave me a job in her shoe store – a job that kept me out of trouble, taught me how to manage a business, deal with difficult people, and help me become the strong person that I am today.

Sadly though, as much as I was able to successfully change my mindset and most areas of my life, one part didn't change – I continued to be a victim in my marriage. On the day that I reached my limit (I'd had enough), I officially left my marriage.

After my divorce, I set limits for what was allowed (or not) in my life; I set boundaries – and enforced them; I began to respect myself and in so doing, I gained respect from others. It took me a long time to understand this *life-policy*; before that, I felt undeserving of friendship and lasting relationships.

* * *

In 2011, I was diagnosed with early stage cervical cancer. Devastated by the news, I kept it hidden from everyone, but my mother (who is my confidant and my best friend). Thankfully, the cancer cells were non-malignant; however, it meant that my surgery was deemed a non-priority and that I waited ten months before it took place.

From the time I was diagnosed to when I had surgery, I maintained my work routine and commuting schedule, but otherwise kept to myself. At home, I lived like hermit, neither seeing nor interacting with anyone.

Tired and drained, I was alone and very unhappy. I avoided asking close family and friends for help with household chores, and my daughters. With no one by my side, I relied heavily on my girls for everything; I burdened them with my impatience, fragility, anxiety, demands and neediness.

In April 2011, my surgery took place. The dark clouds vanished and my merry life resumed. The glory lasted all but seven days. One week later, I was hit by a car going so fast that it hurled through the air like a projectile. I hit the ground like a sack of potatoes.

I have no idea what possessed me to continue on like a trooper. Immediately after being carried to the hospital and having my wounds assessed (at the time I thought I was okay), I returned home and immediately phoned my boss to tell him what had happened. I advised him that I'd need time off.

The next day, I felt energetic and invincible; however, the following morning, when I tried to get out of bed, I fell immediately to the floor. Not knowing what happened, my heart raced in a panic. I wanted to scream, but couldn't. I wanted to get up – my legs wouldn't work! Never in my life did I felt so helpless. "If only I could get to the phone," I thought. It was out of reach. Then it occurred to me, who would I call anyway? I didn't have any *real* friends.

That day ended up being a turning point in my life. Because I kept repeating my pattern of isolating myself from others, I was put into a situation where I HAD to ask for help and HAD to start doing the deep work of healing my emotional hurts.

Relying on people to help me relearn to walk, talk, and improve my short-term memory was the hardest thing I've ever done. During this time, I began to let my guard down so that people could see the *real me*.

In the ten long months before my cancer surgery, I built a strong friendship with a woman on the bus that I commuted to and from work on. When she learned of my car accident, she immediately contacted me and shared that she had had a brain tumor, been operated on, and survived. She said that if she could beat the odds, I could too.

To help me relearn to spell and count, we'd get together each week to play Scrabble. If it were not for this friendship, I know in my heart that I wouldn't have made it. I would have ignored the need to ask for and receive help from others, and I'd still be sitting on my couch, overweight and miserable as hell.

To this day, I am grateful this woman stuck by me through thick and thin; especially during my good and bad days when I felt angry and discouraged.

During the two years I spent recovering and healing myself emotionally, I had a lot of time to reflect.

I realized that when it came to being violated, as long as the other person wasn't willing to take responsibility for their part in the situation, no matter how much I wanted it, it would never be fully resolved. I needed to let stop letting the situation take me down. Healing takes time. The best way to move on was to take responsibility for healing myself, change my mindset by seeking assistance of qualified professionals, surround myself with the right individuals, participate in support groups, and reach out for help to learn and grow.

Any time my mind drifted into thoughts of, "I should have said this...or I should had done that..." I came to realize that these thoughts were stealing energy away from my body. My healing was not only about where I wanted to be, it was about the journey and correcting my course along the way.

As soon as I started speaking my truth (without shame, or blame) about what my violator had done, my body and soul started feeling at peace. It was exhilarating and liberating, like a huge weight had been lifted off of my shoulders.

As I walk my path in day-to-day life, I continue to have an amazing journey of ups and downs. I see now that what's made the biggest difference in my life is my attitude about each situation that I'm in.

No matter what is happening in my life, it's my mindset that sets me free each and every time.

Joanne Allaire is a Certified Operational Business Analyst with Justice Canada, former athlete in several sports and artist at large. She owns a growing Financial Company, is a Leadership Entrepreneur and contributes to the aging and disabled community. She is an effervescent individual, incessant reader, learner, and "teacher" in many aspects of life.

Joanne has a diverse range of experience in areas like: franchising, commercial acting, catering, public servant in various minister's offices, architect, engineers, gold mining, dance teacher, and marketing and sales representative. In a nutshell, Joanne is inspired by everything she touches and is a model to the saying "You can achieve anything."

Email: Jo4leader@gmail.com

Twitter: @jo4leader

CHAPTER 7 RACHEL LEDUC

Dear Diary, I met a man...

2002

Dear Diary, For the past few weeks, I've been chatting up this guy named "M" on a dating website. I have to admit that right now I'm a little perplexed – I'm forty and he's twenty-eight. He's twelve years younger than me and he keeps chatting me up. What's up with that?

Okay yeah, his online dating profile looks good and by his photo, he's decent-looking. Still, I'm wondering if something's wrong with him. I mean, I'm twelve years older – I clearly listed it in my profile. I have no interest in dating a younger man. He should know better. I'll keep the conversation light and eventually, he'll go away."

* * *

2003

Dear Diary, I can't' believe that after twelve months, "M" is still chatting with me. He wants to meet me. I wonder what is wrong with him? Can't he see the age difference?

* * *

July 2, 2004

Dear Diary, Guess what? "M" turned thirty in May! He should be old enough now to realize that I'm way too old for him and that we're in totally different stages of life. You know what? I'll go on a date with him, so he can FINALLY see it with his own eyes.

July 7, 2004

Dear Diary, I really didn't feel like going for a drink with "M", but today I gave in. He's definitely patient – at this point he's been wanting to meet me for two years. I decided to meet up with him with the idea of cutting it short. Four hours later, I found myself thinking, "Hmmm...he's extremely good looking, open-minded, non-judgmental, calm, intelligent, and to top it all off, he's a gentleman.

I think I'll see him again.

* * *

December 31, 2004

Dear Diary, Wow! Already six months with my Boy Toy! Who would have thought?

* * *

Spring 2005

Dear Diary, This man amazes me! When I'm with him, I feel relaxed and I'm the real me. I'm not even scared of being rejected or judged. I don't need to be a powerful businesswoman. I can actually let go, be vulnerable, and have fun.

It feels good that we can play and laugh together. I wonder where this "relationship" is going.

* * *

Spring 2006

Dear Diary, "M" and I started out as friends and it turned into "friends with benefits". What I'm actually shocked about is that things between him and I have actually blossomed into a heartfelt love affair.

I'm still surprised that a man twelve-and-a-half years younger is the one who's helping me to break down my walls and deal with the years of relationship baggage that I've been carrying around. I wonder if this is why he came into my life. This guy gets me and I get him. When I'm with him, it's like being on a deserted island, where it's just the two of us and nothing else matters.

* * *

2007

Dear Diary, Even though we accepted the age difference, we are at different stages in our lives. "M" is mixed up in his head and his heart – he thinks that he might want to have kids.

For as long as I can remember, I've wanted a child, but no babies for me; my 2006 surgery closed that door. I'm pretty sure he'll figure out that he actually WANTS a family and that I can't do that for him. I'm pretty sure that one day, we'll need to say goodbye and move on. I think in his heart, he knows it too.

* * *

2008

Dear Diary, People around us don't understand that "M" and I actually have a great relationship. Years of sharing weekends, vacations, and holidays and not living together, or planning a long-term future doesn't make sense to them.

Even though we both know the relationship will end, "M" and I decided we'll ignore people and take things one-day-at-a-time. All that matters is that it works for us. I'm doing my best to live in the present, and not think about what'll happen in the future.

* * *

September 2009

Dear Diary, He finally said, "I love you!" Over the past five years, he's seen every side of me, my feminine side and my masculine side; he loves all of me. What a beautiful gift.

* * *

Fall 2010

Dear Diary, I can't believe we are still connected. We tried to part but we always get back together. We must love each other more than I realize.

* * *

May 2011

Dear Diary, I am sad. "M" met another woman. He has no idea where it's going, but he needed to tell me.

When I told him that he wasn't allowed to call, email, text, or see me anymore, I felt really bad; he actually got tears in eyes and asked, "You no longer want to be my friend?"

If he and I stay in touch, this potential relationship and the new girl will never have a chance. It's best for him and possibly for me (even if I don't see it now) to let go.

Breaking-up is really hard. We cried. I appreciate that he was able to show me that he was hurt and express himself. Men tend to think that they need to display strength all the time; often they don't realize that it's a blessing when they share their true feelings with a woman.

* * *

November 2012

Dear Diary, My hair has always been my thing. I need to let go of so many things and I don't' seem to be able to. Today I shaved my head. I am sure that letting go of my hair will help me let go of all the rest.

It's been eighteen months since "M" and I went our separate ways, and I'm just starting to feel better. I feel proud, that I was able to set him free so that he could go on to have the life he wanted and needed.

I believe that true love is wanting for someone else's happiness even if you're not part of it.

* * *

January 2013

Dear Diary, "M"'s grandmother passed away. At the funeral, I met the new woman in his life. It wasn't easy. It's been a year since he and I have seen one another – I was really nervous. I thanked the new woman for being in his life and for helping him fulfill his dreams.

* * *

Today

Dear Diary, I no longer see or talk to "M" on a regular basis. When a break up happens because of a fight and negative feelings, the new person doesn't feel threatened by the ex. Because we ended our relationship with love and comprehension – I totally understand and respect his wife's wishes that he and I not to see each one another.

One thing I do like however is the great friendship I still have with his mother. She and I speak on a regular basis and travel together any time we get the chance to. I'm really grateful that "M" is fine with it.

The relationship "M" and I had allowed me to learn a lot of valuable lessons as I move forward in life. I have learned to appreciate the people in my life and express how I am feeling about them without fear. With "M", there were times I held back my feelings, thinking it'd hurt less when it ended. I regret not taking full advantage of every moment and saying how I really felt in my heart.

I also learned that I can't just accept any man into my life; he needs to have qualities that allow for both people to grow. The person I least suspected was the one who taught me the biggest lessons about love.

Ending the relationship also allowed me to go on and discover my purpose in life. If I were still with "M" I wouldn't be an Ambassador for Women's Potential, or living in the Dominican Republic right now. I would be in Ottawa, hating winter and likely resenting it.

Our soul always knows what's best for us. We just need to step back from our fears and judgements and let its message be heard. We don't always understand why we are where we are, or doing what we're doing, but if the message comes from our soul, then it's what it should be. This is true for all situations – there are no exceptions.

"M" was able to fulfill his dreams of having a big church wedding, a honeymoon in Hawaii, and starting a family. He now has a beautiful baby boy. When I told him about sharing a part of my diary about us in this book, he said, "Everything about you and I was good and I only have positive things to say about our relationship. Go ahead. I trust you."

I'll always be very grateful that our paths crossed and I thank the Universe for the gift of this amazing man in my life.

Accomplished business woman, Rachel Leduc Author, and Speaker. Dedicated to women's well-being and making a difference, Rachel's teachings help women achieve their goals through balanced, healthy lifestyles and taking practical steps to achieve the life of their dreams.

To give women opportunities for showcasing their passions, businesses, and hobbies, Rachel coordinates the annual "You Deserve It!" Conference for Women and has developed an extensive variety of women-only training, events, and trips.

Rachel travels the world sharing her ultimate life mission - that all women know **they ARE more than enough!**

Website : www.RachelLeduc.com

Facebook : Rachel Leduc Public Figure

CHAPTER 8   SUZIE HOLLIHAN

My Beacon in the Night

I am his lighthouse. He knows that even in his darkest and bleakest of times, I will be there.

Because that is what you do.

I pulled a quote out tonight by Maya Angelou from a pack of cards, "Have enough courage to trust love one more time. And always one more time."

I have. Always that one more time.

It has been hard. Thirty one years and many of those nights sleep was elusive – from crying, or fear – as I knew he was hiding outside down the street. Many days I have spent venting, or sobbing to anyone who would sit still. We've had to implement a safety plan that involved the neighbors – just in case. We have fled many times in the night to escape his wrath. I have lived in a crisis shelter. I have stayed hidden in motels, until his anger subsided. That was our life.

And I have found him many times, alone, crying, drunk, and hungover and supported him. I have yelled, screamed, begged, cried, threatened, and even laughed at his antics. I have tracked him down when he was suicidal by keeping him on the phone, saying *one of our children was seriously hurt,* until the police could find him and get him help. I have dragged him back to his apartment when I found him downtown, so drunk he didn't really know me.

And I always tried to do it one more time – and then, once more. He has left many times, when the pressures of a busy family were too much for him to bear; too much to think about in his already swirling brain. He has left for minutes, days, weeks and years, and he has always come home with a grin and a shrug, and his blue eyes shining with tears.

Why? Because he knows I will be here. His children will be there. Because that's what family does. And that's what family stands for. We always knew that he "had our back." Even in his lowest times, we knew that if we needed help, he would try to be there. Because deep down in his soul, he loves us. We saw the pain and the struggle, and how he was unable to control his outbursts, or impulses. The many pills he was on would make him sick, or send him to a place we were not allowed into. The alcohol only served to enhance those moments.

And although we begged, pleaded and threatened, he struggled with turning his back on that lifestyle. It seemed nothing would work out for him. He always wanted the best for us, but then he'd have another setback which would send him further away.

I have never been able to turn my back on him. I met him on my birthday. He was *a gift* he tells me and that I can never return him. (I did ask him parents to take him back many times, but instead, I have his father living with me now!)

He is bipolar, with manic episodes that send him flying – literally back to Newfoundland, Canada where he is from. I would get a phone call that he wasn't at work, but instead had taken a flight back *home*. A few days later, he would call and beg me to get him back home.

He has never been able to fully unpack his clothes, and keeps them in a bag in our bedroom ready to flee. He never will. He just needs the option. For many years, he drove around with them in the trunk of his car.

And when I tell my story, people are incredulous. I am not desperate or lonely. I have a very complete life. I own a magazine. I work with youth at risk. I have raised four very successful children. I laugh often and can always find the humor in a situation. And I get him. And sometimes he gets me.

That is enough.

I do not put up with his abuse. I call him on it, or call the police – and charge him. It's a tough road for both of us. He is on medication and when it works, he's fantastic and charming, and the funniest person I have ever met. And when the medication doesn't work, he has to leave. I do not let anything slide. I can't.

He needs me to confront him when I see him going into a downward spiral. I won't let him get away with anything, because this is our vow to one another.

To live with a man who has **ADHD**, an Obsessive Compulsive Disorder and is Bipolar, you have to be strong, and have a sense of humor. You have to be able to laugh at his habits and quirks. We have no secrets between us, or our children. Everything is out in the open. That is what makes it work.

Two years ago, I gave him an ultimatum for the first time. He could either choose to be involved in our lives, or continue on drinking. I would not watch him die and neither would my children. Although he had not been living with us for many years, we still made sure he was fed and involved in our lives. He would call in the night, lonely and scared; and I would talk with him until he fell asleep (terrified he would give up and commit suicide). HIs children would deliver food and make sure he was still alive. We refused to give up on him.

I held my alcoholic mother as she slipped away from us. She was only fifty-nine, but a childhood of abuse led to a lifetime of drinking, and she bled to death one night in my arms. Even love couldn't save her. I vowed then I would not go through it again. Growing up, alcohol had always been a factor in my life.

There were many fun times with my mother; impulsive outings, lots of guests, parties with laughter. She was always the jokester. But, there were many more times that others didn't see – her laying on the floor, sobbing after my father left, or attempting suicide and having to be rushed to the hospital. The sad face of the clown.

I knew I wasn't strong enough to do it again. I was turning out the light. I was ready. I couldn't see the pain in his eyes anymore. I couldn't look in the mirror and see the swollen eyes stare back at me. I guess there comes a time when you're on the brink and not sure which way to go. I knew that afternoon I could not be let down anymore with false promises, or scared by his many drunken threats. He had worn me down.

I am not sure what happened to him the next day, he was driving back to his apartment – drunk – stopped on a bridge, threw his beer out, and called me the next morning to get help. It was the first time since he was teenager that he was able to reach out for support. We drove him to rehab; he swore and told us to never visit. Three days later, after he had dried out enough to use the phone, he begged us to come visit. And we all did. His entire family.

He came home after his rehabilitation – the man we loved. Although fairy tales are supposed to have a happy blissful ending, there will always be the ups and downs associated with having a manic husband. At least, without the alcohol in his system, the medication has a chance to work.

He and I will always struggle, but we laugh often and dance at home. As a family, we get together a few times a week, and with seventeen of us, it ends up being like a circus. Not a day goes by we don't thank God for allowing him to come home. He got his life back and so did we.

I have many scars to remind me of his anger, and we talk about it sometimes, but not often. That part of our relationship is over. We left it behind as we started a new journey – but we've never forgotten. I will never trust him completely – he knows that; but I will always try to understand what he is going through. I promised him that. That was the most I could give.

And I hope that my children, or others, will not see my sticking by him as an act of meekness, but rather one of courage. Of believing that every person deserves to have love, and that a person does not inherently want to hurt others. Sometimes, stuff gets in the way and you need a light to guide you home.

Suzie Hollihan is a dreamer, planner, and doer. She co-owns a bi-monthly magazine, has published books, teaches sewing and quilting, and works as an educator in a program for Youth-at-Risk. Her many-faceted careers have been in advertising, retail stores, sewing instructor and trainer, owner of a textile factory and freelance writing. Life is never dull in the Hollihan house! Throw in five children, five of their spouses and six grandkids, a Saint Bernard, and you can imagine Sunday night dinners at her house. Her motto: "What a crazy week coming up and I love it!"

Email:hollihan@rogers.com

CHAPTER 9   MARIA SOWDEN-WEINGARDEN

The Decisions That Changed My Life

It's a beautiful, warm, sunny summer morning and I'm sitting in my gazebo sipping my morning latte, reflecting on my past.

I was born in a small village sixty kilometers south of Rome, Italy. My parents were simple folk and had a loving marriage.

My dad was a handsome young man and my mom was beautiful, with jet black, wavy hair, sparking brown eyes and a warm smile. Being eight years older than my mom, by the time Papa and my mom met, he'd been engaged twice. Papa said his previous girlfriends were nice, but the day he met my mom, he knew instantly that she was the one he'd been waiting for.

I was two years old when my dad immigrated to Canada. Two years later we (my mom, me, my paternal grandmother, and my dad's youngest sister) boarded a passenger ship and followed him.

On May 4th (my fourth birthday), we docked in Halifax and boarded a train. Hours later, we arrived in Ottawa - our new home.

Adjusting to a new country was extremely difficult. All that had been familiar to me was gone. I missed my maternal grandparents and the other family members we'd left behind. I missed our tiny village where we all knew each other. I missed playing hopscotch with my friends. I missed going on evening *passigiatta* (strolls) with my family.

One morning, I was sitting on my front porch, and saw a woman with two little girls around my age, walking down our street towards my house. As they approached, one of the girls looked my way, smiled and waved. I waved back and they walked on. I felt happy that I'd met someone.

The next morning, I sat on my front steps again, hoping to see the little girl.

And I did.

As the woman and little girls neared my house, one of them smiled and waved again, but this time, she ran over to me and started speaking in English.

I didn't know English and couldn't understand her. Not knowing how to respond, I simply smiled and waved.

The third day, the little girl ran over to me again, climbed the steps, and sat down beside me. Her name was Jeannie and she was my first real friend.

Jeannie taught me my first English words, and introduced me to new foods, games, and toys. A few months later, Jeannie and her family moved away. On the day she left, we clung to one another and cried. I never saw Jeannie again, but am still thankful for her friendship and for how she reached out to me.

I started school at the age of six. As the only one in my class who didn't speak English, the kids would point, whisper, and laugh at me. I didn't understand what they were saying, but knew they were making fun of me.

On many occasions, I'd place my head down on my desk, cover my face and burst into tears. I felt confused, lonely, and disconnected from the other children. It was here that seeds of unworthiness were planted.

My parents were very protective and money was tight. Because of this, I never had the experience of going to movies, playing with the latest toys and gadgets, or going camping and travelling like my friends did.

I remember the first time I was invited to a sleepover. My mother thought it was the strangest idea ever.

"Why would you want to sleep at someone else's house?" she asked.

My mother didn't understand how much fun a sleepover could be; never having experienced it herself, I wasn't allowed to go.

At sixteen, I met a young man (my future husband).

In strict, traditional Italian families the woman's role is to marry, raise a family and care for the home. Where dating is concerned, the man asks the woman's parents for permission to date her. In my case, permission to date me was requested and granted.

"Dates" for my boyfriend and I consisted primarily of dinner and movie nights with my family. If my parents left the room for any reason, my younger sister was instructed to stay with us until they returned. The only private moments my boyfriend and I had were being permitted to go for occasional, short walks around my neighborhood.

Twelve months later, he and I were engaged.

My fiancé was moody, controlling, and prone to outbursts of anger. When I threatened to break off our engagement, he'd apologize profusely and promise to change his behavior.

I was unhappy. He and I didn't have much in common and had completely different outlooks on life. When we discussed our future, my fiancé told me that once we started a family, I would not be allowed to work outside the home, or have a career.

I was shocked.

I broke off our engagement several times. Each time, my actions resulted in a family argument.

"Why are you being so difficult?" scolded my mom. "If you break off the engagement, what will our family and friends say?"

When I tried to explain my position – that I was unhappy and NOT ready for marriage – I was told that things would improve once my fiancé and I married.

In my heart I didn't believe this, but didn't want to create ripples, or disappoint my parents. So I kept my truth locked inside of me.

Two months after my 18th birthday, I was married.

Two months after the wedding, I discovered that I was pregnant.

Three weeks later, I miscarried.

It was an emotional time. Although I mourned the loss of our child, part of me was relieved - I wasn't ready to become a mother.

I became pregnant a second time and miscarried again.

After the second miscarriage, I was profoundly unhappy, disillusioned and depressed. My future looked bleak and hopeless. I asked myself the same questions over and over:

"How am I going to spend the rest of my life married to a man I don't love, whom I have nothing in common with? How can I continue going through the motions of life when I feel empty inside?"

Many times I considered leaving, but then I'd reconsider. Where would I go? How would I support myself? How could I inflict that kind of pain on my parents?

I felt trapped and miserable.

The breaking point for me happened three months after my second miscarriage when my husband INSISTED that we get pregnant again.

In that moment I thought, "This isn't the way I imagined my life unfolding. There's more to life than what I'm getting. I have to get out!"

I vowed to break free from my current circumstances and make that change.

The "change" I made led me into my second relationship, an affair with a man who was also unhappily married.

One day, we each packed our suitcases, left our spouses, and began our journey together. We eventually married and had a beautiful daughter.

My actions created a tsunami of shock within the Italian community. I was shunned, ostracized, and branded a slut. Extended family members declared that I was no longer a member of the family.

The seeds of unworthiness that had been planted as a young girl – a girl who'd been ridiculed, laughed at and ignored – now took root and led to many years of approval-seeking, low self-esteem, and self-doubt.

My second marriage lasted nineteen years. Our first few years together were relatively happy, but eventually the relationship began to crumble. I was restless, wanting to spread my wings, pursue a career, learn and become all that I was meant to be.

I started reading self-help books, attended personal development classes, and considered pursuing higher education. As I became more self-confident, independent and empowered, the connection between my husband and I diminished and the tension between us increased.

Again, I felt held back and stifled. I couldn't face going through another break-up and this time, I had a daughter to consider. I was determined to stick it out and make things work; however, when the pain of staying in an unhappy situation became greater than the pain of leaving, I made the difficult decision to end my marriage.

What followed was a ten-year period of self-discovery, reinvention, tapping into my inner power and finding my voice. Every challenge I endured provided valuable insights that helped shape me into the person I am today and prepare me for my life's work.

Today I'm married to my "forever husband". After going through my own journey of healing and renewal, I am committed to helping women navigate difficult life transitions, heal their wounds, reclaim their power, overcome adversity, and let go of limiting beliefs so they can reach their highest potential.

There have been starts and stops along the way; however, I continue to remind myself that I'm a work in progress. I'm forever evolving and committed to keep moving forward no matter what challenges lie ahead.

Maria Sowden-Weingarden is a Transformation Coach, Law of Attraction Facilitator, Workshop Leader, Energy Healer, and Speaker. She has a passion for inspiring people to realize their full potential both personally and professionally.

A key component of Maria's coaching practice is supporting people through life transitions. Maria is no stranger to navigating change and accepting loss in her own life. After going through her own journey of healing and renewal, she is committed to helping others heal from their wounds, recapture their health, reclaim their power, overcome adversity, and let go of limiting beliefs so they can reach their highest potential.

LinkedIn: www.linkedin.com/in/transformationcoach

Twitter: https://twitter.com/MariaSowden

My Life as a Turtle – How I Finally Broke Out of My Shell

In the Native culture, the turtle totem means walking our path in peace and sticking to it with determination, persistence, emotional strength, and understanding.

I was born into a family of six and a life of adversity. I almost died at birth and required several blood transfusions. Despite the initial challenges in my first few days of life, a prince watched over me... Doctor Prince. I always say that a Prince saved my life, it's so romantic! I survived and my mother took me home. But my challenges continued...as a child, I was often sick.

My dad was an alcoholic and this caused the demise of my parents' marriage. They divorced when I was eight, and my Mom moved us to a small town away from where my Dad lived. Even so, while growing up, I chose to spend a lot of time with my Dad, as opposed to my brothers who chose not to see their father very much.

Even though I stayed with my Dad a fair amount, I never felt very safe. Every weekend, he'd get drunk until he passed out. Many times, I walked the streets until I knew he was asleep. My Dad eventually stopped drinking and he was the best father a girl could ask for.

So why didn't I mostly stay with my Mom? Onto the next issue—abusive environment. Two of my brothers were extremely abusive. Most days were filled with name calling, belittling and extreme violence. While it's true my brothers treated me like one of the boys; they forgot I was a girl. Their treatment psychologically scarred me to the point where I believed that I was worth nothing. Did my mother support me? Not really, I always felt that she preferred my brothers, not to mention she's always been very critical of me. Our relationship has been one that's strained. Some good, some bad. And what about my sister? That's a story for another time.

It was in my youth where I learned to hide in my shell. Thankfully, I had one brother who was gentle and kind with me and because of this, I named my son after him.

As a teenager, I started drinking and doing drugs. My mental, spiritual, and emotional state were so depleted, that I was often depressed, to the point where I tried to kill myself. So many times I prayed for death.

The first time I tried committing suicide, I'd swallowed pills then walked to a nearby park. As I sat on the bench in a drugged out stupor, praying for death to arrive, a voice so loud and clear told me, "*Go to the hospital!*"

I looked around. No one was there.

The voice said again, louder, "*Go NOW! Run!*" – And I did. I remember running so fast that I didn't feel my feet hitting the ground. Was it adrenaline, the high from the pills, or an Angel helping me out? It felt like an Angel; however, because of my unstable and violent childhood, it was hard for me to believe that there would ever be someone or something out there who'd watch over me.

At seventeen, I was seeing a counselor who encouraged me to share my thoughts and feelings (imagine that). I had become so conditioned to being abused and ignored; the idea of talking about myself was completely foreign to me. It was during this time that my healing began.

At twenty, my life changed. A one-night stand turned into a new journey – I was pregnant. The father of my child was a drug addict and not really involved. My drug addictions were intense. My doctor suggested I go into rehab, but I refused. I told him that I would do it on my own. The first few days of getting clean were tough! Cold sweats, feeling nauseous, and being in total fear! But I did it!

When it came time for my son to be born, he was ready! I delivered him within two hours and he was healthy! I felt the presence of God in the room! When I met my son, my precious little gift for the first time, I finally understood what love was. My son's biological father decided that he wanted to be involved in his son's life, but his heavy drug use made that impossible – he was unreliable and violent.

I fought for sole custody for over three years. In the final week of court, I was terrified! I prayed that my helpless baby would be safe. For three consecutive nights, Archangel Michael appeared in my bedroom. At first, I thought I was dreaming. *(No, I wasn't on drugs...He really did appear!)* The final night he appeared, he stood over me and a feeling of peace washed through my entire body. The next day, the Judge gave me full custody of my son. My son was safe!

As a teenager, my son went through his own challenges with drugs and drinking. There was an eight-week period, where I received weekly calls from the hospital telling me that my son had tried to commit suicide.

The last time my son tried to take his life, I was sitting outside of the hospital alone on a bench, when suddenly a woman approached me and asked to sit down. Even though there were plenty of other empty benches around, I nodded *yes* and then thought to myself, "Oh great! Just what I need. A weirdo!" The woman proceeded to say, "He'll be a good man." Then she stood up, walked down the street and vanished. I had a good cry, gathered up my strength and went back into the hospital.

When I walked into the hospital room, my son said to me, "Mom, I need help." (In that moment, I knew that Angels had been at work). As soon as he was discharged from hospital, my son entered rehab and began his journey to a better life.

When my son completed rehab, we decided to make salsa. We coined the recipe "Chrisalsa" and turned salsa making into an annual tradition. Our salsa reminds us of those times and to be thankful that we can make it together every year! My son has since become a father to a beautiful daughter and is following his passion in life. I'm so proud of the man my son has become.

Through all of the challenges with my son's biological dad, I met my husband; we met when my son was less than a year old. We talked and laughed a lot. We were married for seventeen years.

Ten years into our marriage, my husband had a nervous breakdown and his character changed drastically. We tried counseling, but nothing helped. He drank a lot and our home became a toxic environment. I thought I was equipped to deal with it, given what I'd already been through in life.

Wrong!

I gained weight, became diabetic, and fought depression. I left my marriage, filed for bankruptcy and rebuilt my life. I had a nervous breakdown. I felt like a failure. I had worked so hard to have a good life and it was all for nothing! All of my successes meant nothing. I was broke, lost my home, and I had lost most of my possessions. Most of my family wasn't there for me and only added drama for me during one of the lowest times of my life. I have since left anyone who doesn't live in the light.

Desperate. Isolated. Fearful. Confused. Saddened. Angry; all descriptions of how I felt more times than I care to remember.

We've all been there, some more than others. But, in time, I soon realized that I was definitely not alone. Whatever you're going through, know that it WILL pass.

During the difficult times, having a healthy mindset kept me sane. I embraced my authentic self, exercised, made sure I ate healthy and stayed positive. I embraced the love that came my way and I always tried to be kind. I also forgave the people that hurt me, even though they may not be in my life. There's freedom in forgiveness. Angels have helped me in my darkest hours. Knowing this, it encourages me live a healthy life and bring love and kindness to those around me. In turn, love is returned.

Going back to the turtle...I once hid in my shell and carried baggage in my shell; I was slow at times, but agile and quick at others. My shell was sometimes heavy and at other times it was light. My shell protected me.

I got a tattoo of a turtle on my ankle – it's my stamp of pride and personal reminder that I'm finally at home within my shell.

Brigitte Lord's journey has not always been an easy one. At age 47, with a lot of soul searching, she finally feels that she has come home within. Through one of her dark times, Brigitte found peace in the arts - something that kept her occupied, from becoming a passion to a successful business. Brigitte hopes to inspire others to find peace within and embrace the essence of who they are.

Brigitte designs and creates beautiful greeting cards. Her love of music, romance, beauty and traveling influences the designs of her artwork. Each card becomes a unique and timeless piece.

Website: www.masterworkdesigns.com

Facebook: Masterwork Designs Stationery

INTUITION

Whatever title you give your intuition...a message from God, your Inner Wise Voice, your Higher Self, Source, the Universe...we are all capable of having a deep connection and communicating directly with our Divine Intelligence.

Our intuition is our "go to person" for clear direction on any question we need an answer for, and yet many women are disconnected from the wisdom, peace and sense of well-being it offers them. The interesting thing about intuition is that we have the free will to listen to it, or ignore it.

Are you curious to know what happens when you ignore your intuition, and what happens when you listen to it?

Follow the journey of ten women who describe their experiences with their intuition and the situations that forced them to take it seriously.

CHAPTER 11   JEWELS RAFTER

Having Faith in My Awakened Spirit

One might think that professional psychics know what lies ahead for them in their life journey. Unfortunately, for most light workers, this isn't the case. You see, clairvoyants are very aware of other people's futures, but for the most part, we have absolutely no insight into our own lives. This is quite ironic considering the fact that professional psychics spend the majority of their time looking into possibilities and sharing glimpses of the future with their clients. It is my belief however, that being spiritual means we need to experience challenges and obstacles so that we can better understand life, and become more empathetic so we can guide and support our clients. As a psychic, I've also learned the hard way that following your intuition will always get you through any obstacle or challenge that comes up in your life.

I grew up in a Catholic family with parents who worked hard and instilled strict values. We went to church on Sundays and celebrated holidays as a family; however, I never really felt that I fit in. I was THE rebellious child who challenged religion and going to church (in my mind, we were following man made rules). I often argued that I had no need to prove my spirituality by attending mass to show that I had faith in a Higher Power. I had been hearing and sensing Spirit around me continuously, why go to church? If I wanted to talk with God, I could do that myself! As I grew older, I continued hearing voices and sensing the outcome of events before they occurred.

As time went on my abilities intensified. In my teen years, I often predicted events in my friends' lives. This strange ability scared some people and as a result, a few friends distanced themselves from me out of fear.

Feeling self-conscious and odd, I tried to shut down and hide my abilities as much as possible around others; however, the purpose of my skills became quite apparent on one particular occasion when I was fourteen.

As a young teen, my friends and I would usually hang out at the park and spend our time socializing. One summer evening, my girlfriend was sitting next to me and as I looked at her, an overwhelming feeling of dread washed over me.

"*Tell her to go home.*" a voice said out of nowhere.

I had the inexplicable need to tell her to go check on her mother, but she looked at me like I was crazy and dismissed my suggestions. As the minutes passed, I felt an ache in my chest followed by an overwhelming sense of grief and sadness. I begged my friend to leave right away and go home; she became increasingly irritated by my crazy requests, reluctantly gave in and jogged home. Thirty minutes passed. She did not return. Feeling somewhat curious about what was delaying my friend, I walked by her house on my way home. Parked in the driveway was an ambulance and on the front lawn a crowd of people had gathered.

A sense of sadness overwhelmed me as I walked by her house. I didn't understand why the sight of the commotion made me feel like crying. I continued walking home and assumed that we would speak at school the following day. I hoped we could get to the bottom of all the commotion then.

The next morning, she wasn't at school. I felt nauseous throughout the day and after school, rushed home to call her. She refused to take my call.

Her brother informed me that their mother had suffered a heart attack and had passed away suddenly the day before. As I hung up the phone, I felt my knees go weak. In that moment, I believed that somehow I had caused her mother's death to happen. I vowed at that moment never to use my stupid intuitive abilities again, and I shut them down completely.

The rest of my teenage years were spent trying to ignore any gut feelings and voices that arose. For the most part I was quite successful. I assumed that ignoring my intuition was a positive idea, but unfortunately a life threating situation manifested itself, because of my stubbornness.

When I was twenty, I lived in Montreal and worked at a popular night club four nights per week. It was the type of night club that attracted people from all walks of life. Being young and foolishly confident, I would leave the club alone at 3:00 am and walk home unassisted. My intuition would scream at me to get a taxi, but I usually ignored these feelings and continued on.

One Saturday during my shift, a group of three men attempted to get my attention throughout the evening. Something about this trio made me very uneasy; the hairs on the back of my neck bristled each time they tried to approach me. Any time I looked at them, I felt a dark cloud around them and kept seeing a vision of a knife in my mind.

Minutes before closing, one of the three men walked up to me and roughly grabbed my arm and said, "You think you are too good to speak to me?" I asked him to let go of me and signaled to the bouncer that there was a problem. The man was quickly escorted out of the club, but not without yelling that I would be sorry.

I shuddered and felt a knot form in the pit of my stomach. I proceeded to close up and count my cash float before calling it a night.

A voice in my head kept telling me, "W*ait a while longer before leaving.*" I ignored it. I just wanted to get home quickly and shower off the negative lingering energy.

By 3:30am, I was good and ready to leave the club.

"*Stay inside.*" the voice said again. I ignored it.

As I walked out the front door of the club, the uneasy feeling returned. I looked up and down the street to ensure that the man wasn't waiting outside. The only people around were two drunk women walking arm-in-arm down the sidewalk and a middle aged couple making out against a car.

I let out a sigh of relief and looked for a taxi to take me home. As it was closing time for most night clubs, no taxis were in sight. I walked to the corner of the street to try and hail one passing by. Within seconds, I felt the uneasy feeling again – someone was watching me.

"*Start running!*" the voice in my head boomed. In my mind, I rationalized that it was simply paranoia.

Moments later, two hands grabbed me by the throat and I was dragged backwards into a nearby alley. I struggled to get free, but was punched in the temple and lost consciousness. When I regained consciousness, I was lying on the floor of a motel room. My hands were bound and the three men from the club stood over me.

My body went cold with fear.

All I could think was, "OMG! I am going to die on this floor and nobody knows I am here."

I screamed and one of the men punched my face. My head reeled from the impact. I felt them rip my clothes off as they held me down with a knife.

I spent the next two hours being brutally raped and beaten. Each time I tried to fight them off, they became more aggressive. I stopped struggling and emotionally disconnected from my body. I felt myself float away and prayed for death to happen quickly.

The voice in my head whispered calmly, *"It's not your time to die."*

Eventually, the torture stopped. The three men walked out of the room, leaving me for dead. *"Breathe."* said the voice.

As I took a deep breath, my intuitive gifts flooded in like a lightning bolt. As the tears streamed down my cheeks, I felt grateful to simply be alive.

After the incident, I could see and sense future events instantly.

Today, I embrace these abilities and offer readings to those needing a glimpse into their own future. I realize that following your intuition can change your life drastically and that sometimes the Universe throws us curve balls. These curve balls are not only life's way of keeping us on our toes (which is a gift in itself), they're often life's way of bringing us wonderful surprises. For example, like my surprise of being blessed with being a professional clairvoyant, who has the opportunity to help other women daily.

My biggest takeaways from my experience in the hotel room that day are to ALWAYS listen to the voice inside your head, acknowledge your gut feelings, and open the door to as many meaningful possibilities as you can.

Jewels Rafter is an International Clairvoyant, Medium, Holistic Therapist, and Radio Show Host who has been living her passion for over fifteen years. She is the CEO of Harmony Radio and her own company, Ohm Readings & Therapies. She is a single mom of two beautiful teenage daughters who help to keep her grounded. Jewels specializes in Clairvoyant Readings, Mediumship, and holistic therapies. Her passion is to help people find answers and offer guidance by sharing her gifts. Having faced and overcome numerous personal challenges, she loves empowering women and helping them find their light at the end of the tunnel.

Website: www.ohmreadings.ca

Facebook: www.FB.com/JewelsRafter

CHAPTER 12 MÉLANY PILON

My Inner Wisdom Tells Me Amazing Things

Hi Beautiful! Welcome to your journey! A couple of weeks ago you turned thirty and in your usual, dynamic way you celebrated. You seized what life had to offer, and you went tandem skydiving. Good for you! I admire your courage and craziness. Looking back at you in the mirror, I want to tell you how proud I am of what you've accomplished and what you've been through up until now.

As a young girl, you were this cute bundle of happiness, without worries or any expectation of life – you simply were. As you aged, you became aware of the changes in and around you. You experienced bullying, toxic relationships, grieving, deployments overseas with the military, and many other bumps in the road. Through this, you had your fears and so far, you've conquered them all.

You know the most important relationship you will ever have is with you, and that the key to your life is to find harmony and balance within yourself. Let's take a deeper look inside of you and at all of the love and layers that makes you, YOU.

Self-love through loving your body...

Through your health and feelings, you learned that your physical body tells you what's happening within you emotionally, mentally, and spiritually. You must pay attention to how your body feels; it will tell you when something is good or bad, by showing up as a feeling, or as a physical discomfort.

For example, the physical changes you experienced during puberty were not easy. You started feeling different, you didn't know where, or how to fit in. You cared a lot about what others thought of you, because you wanted to look and be like them. You feared and started questioning yourself and asked,

"What is wrong with me? Am I good enough? Am I pretty enough?" The more you worried, the more you became blocked, engaged in unhealthy habits and gained weight.

Looking back at old pictures of yourself, you see this two hundred pound girl with no self-esteem and no confidence. You were teased and bullied through the first half of high school. One day, you decided you'd had enough – you didn't like the way you looked, refused to live that way, and decided to make changes in your life. With the support of your grandmother, you learned that your body is a reflection of your state of being and that if you're not willing to put the effort on yourself, then your body will reflect just that.

When you realized that no one is perfect, you showed yourself the respect and gratefulness you deserved. You became happier and healthier. You showed love to yourself by honoring and nurturing your body and sticking with your new habits of healthy eating, working out, and treating yourself to a spa day once in a while. When you physically changed, you were rewarded with positive energy. Don't ever be afraid to get out of your comfort zone. If you push your body to its limit, you will see next time that you'll be able to go further and realize that there was never a limit. Push yourself a little bit more today than you did yesterday, so that tomorrow you can go further.

Self-love through loving your feelings...

Your emotional body stores and remembers every emotional experience you've ever had, from the most joyful moments to the most painful ones. For some reason, the emotions connected with negative experiences tend to stick around and leaves residue and inner wounds without you even knowing it. Over time, suppressing all those negative feelings makes you react and behave in ways that don't feel like your true self at all. Letting go of suffering is extremely difficult; that's the reason why people are afraid to be alone with themselves. They will do everything in their power to distract themselves with technology, food, or substance abuse in order to forget.

Remember your high school years? Your insecurities created a lot of negativity in your life. Your negative emotions showed up as physical pain. Nausea and tears were your friends and you started isolating yourself from the outside world to escape the suffering. For you My Love, emotional eating was your crutch and you gained weight because of it. Once you decided to make changes, you had to understand why those feelings were there, face them, and let them go. As painful as it was to feel them, your emotions made you aware of your blockages. It was not easy to forgive the insecurities that came from your negative thoughts about yourself and the classmates who bullied you, but it was the only way to let go of those negative feelings. Now you understand that emotions are temporary and it's easier to deal with them right away. By observing your feelings from a distance, you were more objective and saw them clearly. Everything is neutral; it's your own perception that makes your emotions feel good or bad.

Self-love through loving your mind and thoughts...

You already know that your mental body contains your EGO, and that it takes control of your mind with distractions like daily stress, worries, and fears. Your mental body includes as well your divine mind where you can find peace and stillness.

Our fast paced society and lifestyle make it hard to keep our mind still. We are continually distracted from feeling and living in the present moment. It's crucial that you learn how to slow down and pay attention to your thoughts. Find activities that you love to do, or learn something new; this will help you create your reality with a positive attitude and keep your mind in the present moment. You are what you think.

Think back to high school: You thought poorly of yourself, worried and didn't want to be rejected or left alone. This is what caused you to have emotional insecurities and weight gain. When you decided to not care about what others thought of you, you started to see yourself transform and blossom. Pay attention to your thoughts and be careful of what you let enter your mind. I want you to view your mind as a garden. Anything negative is like a weed; if you don't deal with it right away, it will spread and overtake your mind. Suffering comes from living in the pain of the past, or the fear of the future. Put your attention on the present moment and you'll find peace and balance.

Self-love through loving your connection with yourself...

Your spiritual body is an infinite source of love energy which connects you to everything that exists. *Everything!* For some reason, when you grew up, you lost your connection with the Source. It's still here – blocked off and hidden. In order to reconnect, you have to reach harmony and balance in all of your other bodies (physical, emotional, and mental).

This is the hardest and most painful process you will ever go through. Not everyone is ready to face their struggles; however, once you feel ready, you will be guided one step at a time through life experiences to explore the parts of yourself that need to grow; it won't be easy. The more you are in balance, the more you will spiritually awaken, your consciousness will expand and your perspective will change.

Connection to Source has a wonderful feeling of unconditional love. Remember the day you were looking at yourself through the mirror, and you felt something flowing in and around you with such intensity that it made you cry of happiness and love for yourself? That was it.

Remember to open up. Be honest and vulnerable with yourself. Love is endless to receive and therefore endless to give. Now that you've found Love within yourself, go help others find it within themselves.

Your Eureka

My Love, your happiness depends on you and you alone. Don't try to find happiness outside of yourself. You came to this earth to learn, grow, and live your life. Keep on learning and exploring the areas you've never seen, or been to before; you will be amazed with what you can find out about yourself. There are more beautiful experiences to come. Don't be scared—embrace the change. The choice to be happy is always yours.

Know that you are strong enough to face any situation on your own. No one can stop you from doing what you want to do. Remember that nothing is permanent, and pain is only temporary.

You are a fish in an infinite ocean. You are a bird in an infinite sky.
Follow the flow without any expectation.
Don't question life; you are where you need to be at this exact moment.
You are infinitely powerful; embrace your new awesomeness.

I am honored to be your best friend and remember you are never alone.

Your Higher-Self

At a young age, Mélany Pilon explored the world, as she was born in Moose Jaw, Saskatchewan into a military family and moved several times across Canada. Mélany spent most of her childhood in Ville de Saguenay, Québec. Because she was interested in science, Mélany decided to join the Canadian Armed Forces as a Meteorological Technician straight out of high school. During her eleven years of service, Mélany has been transferred multiple times. She's also been deployed overseas on few different occasions. With all her experience, Mélany is more appreciative of life and has a broader perception of the world.

Email: m.n.melany.pilon@gmail.com
Facebook: www.FB.com/melany.pilon.9

CHAPTER 13   MELINDA HØGVARD

Learning to Live with My Knowing

I was going through a hard time recently and all I could do was ask myself, "Why now?" My wonderful son bypassed the terrible-twos and most of the adolescent angst. We were always in tune with each other, which I considered huge a blessing. So to my surprise, he's picked now – in his early twenties – to challenge me about his upbringing. How could we remember things so differently? Being a single parent is never easy, but this was hard.

I repeatedly found myself sifting through my memories looking for the truth. Painfully, I knew that whatever I found didn't matter, because we each had our own versions of "the truth." So I did my best to not invalidate my son's perspective and tried to be as supportive as possible. Thankfully, our loving and powerful connection remained as strong as ever.

One day, while I was taking a walk, I mulled over my situation. I was preoccupied again which just made me feel heavy, sad, and fed-up. It was a beautiful day, but I barely noticed. My imagination was too busy. I was caught in a mental loop of dark thought, and these negative thoughts kept looping me back into reliving my past. I kept getting side-tracked by this egoic trick and how it was making me feel, temporarily forgetting it was just camouflage from the truth. The ego's job is to keep us in the "known" to "keep us safe" and I got caught out – again.

I wasn't happy and decided in a moment of awareness enough was enough! So as I walked, I asked myself my "go-to" question:

"What do I want?"

I then took a long slow deep breath to clear my energy, and very clearly received a message from my Knowing:

"Be according to who you are, <u>not</u> what you are going through"

Yes, thank you! The message was simple, profound, and exactly what I needed to hear in that moment. It reminded me that I'm not my life circumstances. *I am* an Infinite Being having a human experience. *I am* a creator of my circumstances and *I am* in charge of my energy at ALL times. I felt very thankful for the reminder and gave thanks to my Knowing, acknowledging the message and our connection.

Taking a deep breath when I felt emotional took me out of the dark mental loop I was in. It awakened me into the Present Moment where I could gain clarity. I was out of my imagination and back in the Present – back in *"real life"* – *"my life"* – and I was aware and free again. My senses expanded and suddenly the day was alive and vivid.

So what is my "Knowing?" It's the wisdom that comes to me from my Source. It's very active in my life and comes to me to help me understand myself, the world around me, and all the dynamics being played out.

As Infinite Beings having a human reality, we all have the ability to access and live from our Source. Until we do, we will keep living through our conditioned self. The conditioned self is the part of us that's been layered with the ideas, thoughts, points of view, judgements, and belief systems that we've adopted from our family, society, media, etc. along with habits and the impact of events. The conditioning happens and stays because we haven't been taught another way. It becomes our programming and defines our "identity".

My connection with my Knowing goes back as far as I can remember. It's been the constant thread in my life. It gave me insights like a play-by-play, or running commentary. Being constantly connected has been really annoying at times. Any time I exaggerated, avoided telling the truth, or told a lie, my Knowing would tell me as I was speaking! I never got away with anything growing up! Over time I simply learned to accept it. Thankfully the flip side of this was that my Knowing also pointed out incongruences. Essentially, it was like a built-in radar that told me when others were lying to me or themselves, or they were behaving out of integrity.

My Knowing was also very caring. It helped me through the death of my grandfather when I was nine-years-old by letting me know that even though he was gone, death simply meant he was somewhere else in spirit. As a teenager, my Knowing warned me not to get into a car with friends who'd offered me a lift. Thankfully I said *no*, because soon after that, their car skid off the road and over a bridge and they were all injured.

The relationship I have with my Knowing developed over time. As a child, it was simply there and I never questioned it. Later in life, as my ego developed, I often ignored it – like a teenager ignores their parents. As a young adult, any time I didn't listen to my Knowing, I ended up having "would've, could've, should've" moments. It was also very frustrating when I'd ask a question, and didn't get a response. Actually, my Infinite Self always responded; I simply wasn't "Present", or too busy to hear it. Despite the growing pains with my Knowing, I *knew* and was deeply comforted by the fact that it would always be a life companion. As my relationship with my Knowing grew and developed, so did I.

Today, I consider my relationship with my Knowing and my Source as a collaboration. We are partners in this life. I'm constantly "dialoguing" with my Infinite Self. When I want to know or understand something, I'll casually ask questions like, "What's the truth about this?" "What will it take for this to happen?" "What's possible?" Whatever I want to know, or need help with, I ask and responses come through an instant awareness or through various life situations.

To get to this point, I had to grow beyond my conditioning, live what I was learning and integrate the understanding. To help me make sense of my life, I constantly asked for Truth, Wisdom, and Understanding. As a result, I was called to live these ideals in my own life. Lessons abounded!

One of the lessons I learned is that because part of me is an Infinite Being, I have aspects of *limitlessness* available to me at all times. For years I was a great meditator and I could meditate for hours. This didn't help me much when Life was disturbing my peace by trying to teach me something. I had to cultivate skills to use "on the hoof" and one of these was a simple, but very profound, Conscious Breath strategy that kept me in the Present Moment. Now, when the dramas of life happen, I can let them pass over me like water off a duck's back. This also taught me that I'm the tool I need and that the perfect time to practice would always be now, in the Present Moment – never waiting for planned moments.

My biggest lesson has been around the natural Law of Cause and Effect. It's a law of physics I learned in High School. It states that *for every action there is an equal reaction*. As a child I was intuitive and a keen observer. As a personal game, I'd often predict to myself what would happen next. As an adult, repetitive relationship patterns forced me to wake up from my childhood conditioning and apply this Law to my everyday living so I could live life on my own terms.

I realized that everything I saw around me in the outside Material World were the Effects. These effects could only mirror me; never create or complete me.

Any time I found myself in need of something and went "out there" to "find" it, there wasn't any flow. I'd struggle and end up disappointed. However, whenever I started within and listened to my heart's desires and made choices from there first, I was being the Cause and actively creating my circumstances. There was flow and Life would deliver to me what I needed to make things happen. In one instance, I followed my Knowing to apply to a particular school for my son. The Head Teacher said my son did not qualify and would never get a place. I went within anyway, made the application, and he was accepted.

My life and my connection with my Knowing has been a journey leading me to my Purpose and my Life's work. The parts of my life that once made no sense, and the parts that did make sense were like mismatched puzzle pieces As an adult, I had such an eclectic career skillset and set of interests that I often wondered what I'd be when I "grew up."

I now experience joy when I help women find fulfilment. The kind of joy that happens when they awaken to the truth of who they are and what their own "Knowing" and life journey is communicating to them.

Melinda Høgvard is a "Change Bringer." She uses all that Life brings to her in her work. Through her unique process of understanding "Energetic Dynamics" she puts behaviors and events into a perspective where one can understand the underlying meaning and transition from Pain to Peace.

Melinda's Dream is to make the World a better place by assisting women open to their full expression; to using their unique gifts in the Great Work of their lives so they can help others do the same.

Melinda is multi-disciplined and uses her extensive skillset and experience in her coaching practice to empower others.

Website: www.MelindaHogvard.com

Facebook: www.FB.com/MelindaHogvard

CHAPTER 14   MARLYN FARREL

Magic Happens when I Say "Yes"

My first memory is of lying in my crib looking at a tree outside my bedroom window. Another is of my grandmother. She held me on her knee, filled her hands with soap, washed my hands in hers, and rinsed them under the pump. I can still feel that sensation today.

Our family lived at the top of a hill and a river ran along the bottom of our yard. As a child, I filled my days with climbing trees, playing with clay and our pet magpie, going for canoe rides, and taking my turtle down to the river so he could swim in a rubber tire.

I was in my late forties when I recognized that nature and my gram were my link to my intuition and spirit. Through their loving, I learned to love myself.

There were many years when I did not love and trust myself and it showed up in my body. It was in the mid-fifties and we had moved from one end of the country to the other. We had two small children and a new baby who was born while my husband was away. Without friends or family and Lou away for months at a time, I became depressed and suicidal. Prescribed meds didn't help. I stopped taking them.

Without being consciously aware, I knew to make a change. Hiring someone to be with the children, I went selling make-up one day a week and made enough to pay the sitter. Going door-to-door, I met people, was invited in, got to know them and gradually got better.

This was by no means my last bout with depression. What I discovered though was that isolation is the worst possible thing for depression and connection with people makes a difference; for me it did.

At times in my life I didn't trust my intuition. There were also times when I was so busy trying to please someone else – often without knowing what they wanted, or if they wanted help at all.

In my late thirties, I was diagnosed with and had surgery for cervical cancer. It was a wakeup call for me because I realized once again that I'd ignored my intuition and not been there for me. After surgery, I experienced inner promptings to look at myself more closely and how I was living my life. It was a gift and the beginning of a rich journey of self-discovery.

The process of trusting my intuition became more concrete six years later, after my mother died and I attended personal development training. That decision opened up a whole new world for me and I changed my life. I not only learned about myself, I met amazing women who, even thirty years later, remain an important part of my life.

One day, while visiting a friend at The Haven (a personal and professional development centre on Gabriola Island, BC, where I had already taken a number of programs), I walked down to the water, slipped, fell, and broke my ankle. The accident happened at a time when I'd been wanting to take three, month-long programs, but kept making excuses and ignoring my inner prompting; I was afraid what I'd find out about myself and the changes I might want to make afterward.

I was away from work for months to recover; interestingly enough, this accident gave me the time and space I needed to make a big decision about my future – I would sell my business. Styling hair and owning a salon were two things I was passionate about. When I turned fifty, I knew intuitively I wanted to make a change. I sold the business knowing I did NOT want to know what I'd be doing next, and that I'd say "Yes" to whatever came along next – ONLY IF it felt right in my heart, AND IF I had some fear about it (When it comes to new opportunities, I believe that if I'm not a little scared or excited, then the experience will be too easy and I won't learn from it).

Shortly after selling my business, I heard about Lay Counselor Training, applied, and was accepted into the program. While attending the training, one of the participants mentioned Life Skills and employment Readiness Training (LSER Training). Once again, trusting myself, I said "Yes" – and registered.

Again life happened. Six weeks before the program started, our son committed suicide. I had no idea how to cope. It was like being in a bad dream that I couldn't wake up from.

I returned to the healing power of nature, spending time early in the mornings walking, screaming, looking, and raging behind Elk Lake. It was early fall and the leaves were changing color. It occurred to me that they were falling to the ground to bring new life to other beings – for the first time, I saw beauty in death.

Still grieving the loss of our son, I attended the LSER Training. It was a wise decision – one that led me to say "Yes" to working for the woman who led part of the training. I was hired to facilitate workshops for people seeking new careers after major downsizing. Seeing them move from discouragement to aliveness was a joy for me.

At one point, I spent a weekend alone at The Haven. I woke in the morning with a workshop idea in my head and wrote it down. Now more than twenty years later, I am still leading this inspired program, Inner Wisdom for Women.

Following the voice inside of me is something I learned to trust many years ago as a participant in a program outside Seattle. There were about forty people taking part; one of them was a young man. I saw him across a circle of silence and we never spoke.

A few months later, I saw a card in a shop and thought, "I should send it to that young man." My Inner Critic loudly told me, "You are a crazy old lady. He won't even know who you are! Don't be ridiculous!" The voice in my head continued even as I mailed the card. And then it was too late, I'd mailed it.

A week later, I got a call from L.A. – from that young man saying he had come home to commit suicide, read my card (which had arrived in the mail that day), and didn't do it. It's hard to imagine that the voice that prompted me to mail the card was the voice I used to ignore...the voice of my intuition.

After working for ten years in the employment field, the program contract ended abruptly. I'd found out about it during a coffee break and was in shock. I'd just started teaching a new group, and after break told them about the change and that I would join them as a leader and participant in the program. At the next break, I called a company that did computer training and when they offered me training, I said, "Yes." This training has served me well over the years.

Six months later, still in shock at losing my job, I got a call from one of the men who had been a participant in the Life Skills training program. He told me that his company needed someone to fill in as receptionist for two months. When I said, "I've never done that before." he replied "You can do it." I said "Yes."

When my time there was almost finished, the woman who ran the employment program asked if I would create a Life Skills and Employment program for at-risk-youth. I said "Yes," then designed, named, and led the program for five years.

The Director of Counseling Services asked me if I would take over a support group for people with mental health issues, for one hour a week. I said, "I've never done that before," and she said, "You can do it, you've got good energy." I said "Yes." Later, I was invited to co-lead a lay counselor training program, which I did for two years.

Ten years ago (again acting on intuition), my husband Lou and I moved to Gabriola Island with our two boxers. Here we found a community of friends who are supportive and loads of fun.

About five years ago, I heard someone say that a mutual friend was taking Creative Journal Expressive Arts Training. The course interested me; I went home, found the web site, and registered. After taking the course, I asked this friend how she liked the training – she had never heard of it.

My grandmother has always been a huge part of my life, even after her death. There are times when I'm leading a program and am unsure what to do – I ask Gram and then I know. Participants have said "There is a spirit in this room" and I agree.

Marlyn Farrell designs and facilitates highly creative and interactive programs supporting growth and learning around our Critics, Career, Inner Child, and Intuition. She has a Diploma in Counseling from The Haven on Gabriola Island, and Creative Journal Expressive Arts and Visioning Coach Certification.

Creativity is the basis for her programs as she believes it is the means to reach deeper levels of awareness. Marlyn brings respect, playfulness, and curiosity to her programs earning her a place in the hearts of participants. She has worked with professionals, mental health clients, and at-risk-youth around career directions and life skills.

Email: marlyn@primalnudge.com

Facebook: Marlyn Farrell

CHAPTER 15   CHRISTY FOSTER

Listen to Your Past to See Your Future

On a cool summer night I stared out my bedroom window. Tears were running down my face as I watched the moon which shone brightly in the endless dark sky. The moon seemed so peaceful and content just to exist. In contrast to that moon, I was definitely not satisfied. Looking back, I realize times of discontent can lead to somewhere better.

Earlier that summer night, I had been attending a church meeting for young women. We lived in a small fundamental religious community where our childhood was very closed and controlled in order to keep us safe from the "world." The leader had explained what the expectations were for us when we became wives and mothers. "You should be more righteous, submissive and obedient to your elders, no matter what," Brother "J" told me and the other teenage girls. "Your purpose on this earth is preordained by God. You were chosen to live this way. Put your feelings and needs aside and do what is right." What was right was to get married young, to have a family, and to not question the leaders.

As I sat on my cold metal chair, I felt sick to my core. Why couldn't I have been born somewhere else? Anywhere but here? Why did God want me to live this way? It wasn't fair!

Walking home from the meeting that night with my friend, my heart had pounded with rage. I told her, "They can say whatever they want, they can't tell me I don't matter. I have every right to say how I am feeling and stick up for myself."

My friend was very quiet. After a few uncomfortable moments she said, "Christy, you shouldn't say things like that!" I wanted to scream and tell her she was crazy. Instead I felt shame and guilt. Shame that I had expressed an opinion that was different than my parents or my leaders. Guilt because I hated every part of my life at that moment and I knew it shouldn't be that way.

Ruby dutifully came back to me later that night. She came not to comfort me, but to warn me. She was just as distressed as I was. We both knew that the direction of my life was at a crossroads.

"I told my Dad about what you were saying," Ruby began. "He said that you had better stop talking like that or no man will ever want you. They will not be able to mold you into what they need you to be."

I was speechless.

I wanted to run away and never come back. Instead, I went upstairs to the solitude of my room.

The other girls in our community seemed to accept our way of life, but I hated the fact that I was never permitted to express how I felt without being judged and criticized. I hated the bubble of fear and doom I lived in. I desperately wanted out of this crazy, suppressed way of thinking. I didn't care if I ever met a man at that point; I would rather be by myself than be molded into something I was not. I knew deep down that I was worth more than just what I could offer someone as a wife. I just kept thinking, *I cannot live this way. I am smart enough to think for myself, and they can't control how I should feel or who I want to be in my life!*

Growing up, I remember looking at other children who were not part of my community and thinking that they looked happy and free, and *I wanted that!* To me *that* meant more freedom, more honesty, more independence; it was a world unlike my own which would provide me with the opportunity to become anything I wanted. I saw no rules out there in the "world." At the time I had no idea how I was going to get *that,* but on this night, I had a whisper of hope that I could find it.

That summer night, looking at the moon through my tears, I knew deep down in my Soul that I did matter regardless of what I had been told. They would not break my spirit. I would fight for me!

Looking back, I see God Moments in my life, moments where God has directed me to something better. My life turned in a different direction that summer night. The events that happened were orchestrated so my eyes would be opened. I was able to see this was not the place for me. Today I have a loving husband, two active sons, an education, a thriving wellness practice, and a personal relationship with God. That beautiful, frustrating summer night was a God Moment.

Two years later, at eighteen, I left the security of my small religious community – the only place I had ever known as home. I left my family and my friends and moved hundreds of miles away to the big city. I stepped away from the shrouded environment of my youth and into a place of many newfound excitement and unknowns. I was determined to find the life I was supposed to live.

I found a place to live, enrolled in beauty school, and began working toward having a better life.

What I didn't know at the time was that uprooting myself from the community of my youth would cause emotional trauma that I would be dealing with for several years. The trauma would manifest itself as physical pain in the form of headaches, severe teeth grinding, stomach aches, and panic attacks.

I became desperate and needed help or I would go insane with the pain and anxiety I kept feeling. I was told about a massage therapist and founder of Myo Therapy. He practiced emotional clearing. I had never heard of emotional clearing, but I had nothing to lose.

I just wanted my health back. I was too young to feel so awful.

I made an appointment with him and he explained to me my body was trying to tell me I needed help. He helped me understand that I was repressing emotions of fear, rage, frustration, anxiety, worry, and low self-esteem. He told me that I needed to examine and deal with these emotions or I would never feel better.

In that moment, I made the connection between thoughts and pain. I was still so angry and hurt and I had not dealt with any of it. Leaving home didn't make the emotions go away. The emotions went right along with me in my suitcase. I now understood, my body had stored all of these strong, painful emotions in the tissues and cells of my body.

I had never dared say aloud that I was angry, hurt, misunderstood, and sad. I had never been given the opportunity to say how I felt or what was on my mind. I judged my emotions as ugly and unimportant. I was so embarrassed to admit I was angry. I had ignored the signals my body was sending me, its aches, its pains, and its fears. But the pain in my body was giving me the message loud and clear: *"YOU MUST deal with your emotional traumas so that you can heal and move on in your life."*

The time in the massage therapist's office that day was another God Moment, just like that summer night. As he worked with me and helped me see and understand myself differently, I knew I wanted to learn how to help others heal too. I had a long way to go, but my path was shown to me that day. I enrolled in the therapy college and my education in therapeutic bodywork began.

I'm fortunate to have a unique insight and perspective from my upbringing that I could not have gained in any other situation. I now know it is possible to embrace parts of ourselves that we once thought awful and grow to love all of it. Our experiences shape us into who we are. I am grateful for where I came from and what I have learned: that it's essential to life to understand the relationship between what the mind "thinks" and how the body is feeling.

Today I have come to embrace my past, present, and future by understanding that I have the right to embrace who I am. On that warm summer night years ago, I thought "Who do you think you are to be different than those around you?" Today I know I am a child of God and by loving myself and having compassion, I make room for others to be who they are. I was born to manifest the light within me and share it with the world.

Christy Foster discovered many years ago that the body sends us messages about our health and well-being. She realized that messages like headaches, insomnia, or acute anxiety were not normal for a healthy person. She sought out help and in the process found her calling in the healing arts.

Now as a Master Practitioner, Licensed Therapist, and Educator, Christy seeks to help others learn the principles and practices behind managing physical and emotional pain. She is teaching others how to heal themselves through the process of Psychosomatic Therapy.

Webpage Link: www.christyfostertherapies.com

Facebook Link: Christy Foster, Salt Lake City

CHAPTER 16   GILLIAN WINDSOR

My Heart Said Yes!

What the hell was I thinking? I didn't come to Greece to end up in another challenging situation. I came to find answers, not create new problems for myself. Gaah!

Feeling vulnerable and exposed in my bikini and sarong and hailing a cab in Rhodes harbor wasn't how I had planned for this day to end. The third cabbie shakes his head no. He isn't going to take the forty-five minutes to drive me back to Lindos either.

What the hell am I going to do? Fear creeps from my gut into my throat, choking my words to the next cabbie. "Will you take me to Lindos?" Another no. A driver yells something to another driver who, muttering something in Greek, opens the rear door of his cab and signals me to get in.

A chill climbs up my spine. *Something's not right.* Doing my best to shake it off, I climb in. What the hell else am I going to do? I scold myself, and recognize I'm in no position to argue or negotiate. I settle in, making sure I'm tucked tightly behind the driver's seat and out of his sight in the rear view mirror. The feeling of unease and tension is still present, and I have no intention of engaging with him.

As we head out of town, I slow my breath and drop into a deeper place within myself in an attempt to sooth my jangled nerves. I shudder, breathe again, and this time I add a little protection prayer to my guides and angels.

This has been a week of roller coaster emotions. Two days ago, I arrived from England to Lindos, Greece, for a week with my close friend. I needed to get away, have some space to clear my head, and take a long hard look at my life. My heart felt like it was in a thousand pieces from loss and grief. My confidence and self-esteem were in tatters. It's a terrible thing to feel alone in your marriage. Coming to Greece was a **brave** act of defiance against the pending ruin of my relationship and my own sense of failure.

As the sun begins to set, I snuggle deeper into my seat and witness the sky dance with the deep evening colors of the closing day. I breathe in the scene with hope of bringing the color and beauty into my heart. My mind wanders back to the beginning of the day.

* * *

"Gillian, do you want to go sailing today?" my friend asks from the hallway of the villa. I walk over to her. She's on the phone with the captain of the yacht she co-owns. "He'll meet you at the beach and bring you back by five o'clock." What a perfect opportunity to shake myself out of my slump. "Yes!" I said enthusiastically. "That would be great. I'm in. This is just what I need."

The Mediterranean Sea sparkles as dolphins play and race alongside our magnificent vessel. Fabulous food and meaningful conversation make me feel almost whole again.

"Gillian, we've come too far to turn around and take you back to Lindos Beach before dark," the captain announces. "We need to continue on to Rhodes." "W-What?" I stammer in surprise. "How will I get back to Lindos?" "There are plenty of taxis to take you," he says. "Oh... Okay, I guess," I mutter to the dolphins.

* * *

My taxi picks up speed as we leave the city borders. The skyline changes to views of the rugged Greek countryside. It's been about twenty minutes since we left Rhodes. I shift a little in my seat so I can watch the sunset continue its colorful dance across the wide-open sky. It's moments like this I appreciate the most. They remind me there is still wonder and awe in the world and I can join in whenever I choose.

I refuse to let the uneasy feeling about my driver dominate my experience. I breathe a little deeper and smile, I will soon be home, enjoying dinner with my friend and sharing stories about our day.

Suddenly, my driver lets out an exclamation. I see him stiffen in his seat.

"NO!" I scream as our hefty Mercedes Benz lifts into the air like an awkward bird deciding suddenly to do aerial acrobatics.

BANG! CRASH! BANG! CRASH! BANG! Over and over we go. Helpless, I bounce around like a pea inside a flying tin can. One more *bang-crash-somersault* and we land roof side down, grinding to a halt in a screech of metal on the side of the road.

Holding my breath I wait. Is it over? Oh my god! Where's the driver? I feel panic rising up. I still think he is going to do me harm, and then it registers that what I'd been dreading has already happened.

I scan the car, looking for the driver, but he's nowhere to be found. Another rush of panic floods through me and I realize I need to get out of this car *now*! What if it blows up?

A new thought then grips me like a vise. I don't know if I have a body to get out with. As this sinks in, I feel a looming dread that I might already be dead. I consider this radical concept for a moment, but the idea I might burn up in this wreck pushes the next thought forward. I wonder what will come with me when I make a move.

I look around the inside of the car and see the back passenger window is wide open. It looks like an easy route out of the wreck. I move toward the opening – *Aaaahhh!* – pain shoots through my body from my neck down to my pelvis. In a strange way it's very welcoming. That answers the question about me having a body or not.

I inch forward and climb through the window onto the side of the road. I crawl as far away from the car as I can. A man appears, I reach out my hand. "Please help me," I plead. He takes a step closer, then unbelievably, he turns and runs away.

Sitting on the side of the road, holding my neck with one hand and my knees with the other, I look again for the driver. Far ahead of me I spot a crumpled lump in the middle of the road. It's him. I begin to shake as shock takes over my body.

Eventually, a car stops and a couple climb out and rush toward me. I grab the woman's arm and plead with her. "Please stay with me. I'm really scared." She stays with me until the police and ambulance deliver us to the hospital and my friend arrives.

My injuries are remarkably minimal in comparison to the magnitude of the car crash. I'm badly bruised with superficial lacerations and a broken bone in my pelvis that will heal without the need of any medical intervention. My emotions, however, are all over the place. I'm in shock one moment and awe the next. How the heck did I survive that accident?

I am told the driver died. We hit an oncoming vehicle that pulled out from behind a tractor. I am also told the "window" I climbed through did not exist. They say the roof of the car was flattened down, squashing anything I could have passed through. I don't have an answer for it. I know what I saw, and I know what I did.

Months turn into years, and life is very different for me since my near death experience in Greece. Coming close to death and surviving such impossible wreckage changed me. The journey taught me to look through the lenses of possibility and potential. It helped me move through the pain of my marriage ending and to create an entirely new life in the United States.

California is beautiful in November. My love and I are driving south on Highway One, and as we go over a pass a beautiful glow illuminates the hills. "Looks like the sun is setting," my partner says. "We should be able to see it in a few minutes." Just ahead, I see the golden red shimmer of the Pacific Ocean. Suddenly, the whole picture is in full view. There in my mind is the reoccurring vision I've been having for months of an exquisite sunset over the ocean. Stunned, I gasp, "Please pull over." I can barely get words out as my body melts into huge puddles of sobs and tears. I feel the magnitude of the journey I've been on since the fateful sunset in Greece.

I've been following a call from deep within myself. It guides me into a profound clarity I know as the energy of my life, my heart, and my soul. I'm learning to trust its movement and signals. In this illuminated moment, as I witness the perfect beauty in front of me, I feel the affirmation that I'm exactly where I'm supposed to be.

I trust the process of my inner and outer journey as I reclaim the vibrancy and fullness of my life.

I'm alive and moving forward.

Gillian Windsor is a passionate lover of life. She continually explores transformation, personal growth, and cutting edge modalities that connect her and others to the magical lightness of Being.

Her adventures include (but not limited to) climbing Mount Kilimanjaro, Tango, Costa Rican zip-lining, a Latin dance performance for 1100 people and meeting Sir Richard Branson on Necker island.

Gillian now lives in Austin Texas with her long suffering husband – she raises his hand to do these things with her, and their white fluffy dog Harley.

Website: www.TheAscendantWoman.com

LinkedIn: www.linkedin.com/pub/gillian-windsor/2/5a0/b32

CHAPTER 17   LIANNE TIBBEN

How Having Faith Gave Me Strength

The summer of 2013 started off like all summers past: plans for camping, summer sports, and family birthday parties. However, God had plans for our family that year beyond what we expected – surprises that would bring our family together and test me in ways I would have never imagined.

July was in full swing, and my dad's health was deteriorating. He was tired and lethargic, and his skin jaundiced. Since birth, Dad had been strong and healthy, never seeing a doctor for anything but a major ear infection. This was the first time I'd ever seen my father in a frail state, and I was scared. When Dad agreed to go for a detailed exam and a battery of diagnostic tests, we were all relieved. What we weren't prepared for were the results.

"What do you mean? Dad has *cancer?*"

My family was devastated and in shock. The prognosis wasn't good. The condition had advanced to the point where Dad required an aggressive surgical procedure called the Whipple. This procedure involved cutting out sections of major organs and most of the piping in between. My Dad was advised by his doctor that out of every one-hundred cases he sees, only twenty percent can be successfully helped. The rest are turned away with no hope. Dad's surgery date was booked for September 25th – two months away.

So my family waited and prayed. We thought about all of the "W*hat-ifs?*" *What if* cancer had spread through Dad's entire body? *What if* he only had months – or weeks – to live? *What if* Mom ended up alone?

Our thoughts of, "*What if?*" were sidelined when Dad's health took a turn for the worst. Within three weeks of his initial cancer diagnosis, Mom phoned 9-1-1 and Dad was rushed into hospital by ambulance. When I arrived and walked into Dad's room, I wasn't prepared for what I saw. "What's going on?" I thought, "This can't be good. Dad's bed and the emergency room floor are covered in blood." I was really scared.

For some unknown reason, dad had lost massive amounts of blood. He was weak and his blood pressure so low, that the doctors were unsure what to do. They administered IV and blood transfusions to try to get his pressure back up.

Our family sat around Dad's bed praying, reflecting on life in silence – Dad was awake, but barely. In a weakened state, he managed to look at each person in the room, holding their gaze for what felt like minutes.

I'll never forget the moment Dad looked at me. I thought, "Is he saying goodbye? God, please don't let this be goodbye."

As Dad was rushed off to the Intensive Care Unit, I prayed for our family to stay strong and for doctors to find a simple fix for what was going on. An hour or so later, the surgeon told us that he'd discovered the culprit—a severe bleeding ulcer that he "fixed". He also shared that Dad would recover.

"Thank you, God, for answering my prayers."

Four days later, Dad came home weak – but alive. After experiencing that dark night in the hospital, Dad's cancer took a backseat for me.

"Lord," I said. "I'm so thankful for each day Dad is alive."

As we waited for Dad's cancer operation date to arrive, his health started deteriorating again. As Dad became increasingly weaker, any slight noise or bright colors became a nuisance. We suspected that he had more than *just* cancer. We prayed non-stop for Dad, for our family, and especially for Mom, his main caregiver.

On operation day, a procedure that should have taken about six hours, took nine. At the end of the day, an exhausted surgeon came to see us and shared that Dad's surgery had gone well. He'd taken longer because he wanted to get each cancer cell. The surgeon also mentioned he'd discovered an infection in Dad's liver and administered antibiotics just before surgery. My family remained silent. We were thankful for the surgeon's confirmation that Dad had something more than cancer and that it was now resolved.

When Dad was transferred to a regular hospital bed, my family and I visited twice a day – love will give you time to do that. As Dad recovered, there were times when his condition seemed to worsen, but in time, Dad recovered and was able to return home.

At home, Dad could walk, but slowly with a cane. He could eat, but only a little. He could hold conversations, but still needed rest. It was great to have him home again. Mom was able to care and provide for Dad, with the love he needed, better than any hospital or other person ever could.

Sadly, the peacefulness lasted only a short time. The day after Thanksgiving 2013, less than three weeks later, I had just spoken with Dad by phone and everything was fine. Minutes later, he called back and asked, "Lianne, will you come over right away? Something is wrong with Mom." When I arrived, Mom recognized me, but her speech was incoherent. I talked with her, asked her short easy questions, and comforted her. Nothing worked. For the first time in my life, I called 9-1-1.

I forced myself to stay strong and not panic when the ambulance attendants arrived and started assessing Mom. At first they thought she'd suffered a stroke but could not confirm as she was responsive to instruction, unlike other stroke victims. I was allowed to accompany mom in the ambulance to the hospital. During the drive, Mom was upset, scared, and suspicious of the ambulance attendant, but calmed down a bit when she saw me.

As the hospital staff took Mom off the ambulance stretcher, she had a major seizure. I was the only family member to see this happen. Each time I think back on seeing my Mom go through it, my eyes well up with tears.

With medication, the hospital staff got Mom's seizures under control, and they started tests to determine what was happening. At first, they thought Mom might have an infection. Since time was of the essence, they immediately gave her a heavy dose of antibiotics. Mom was transferred to a city hospital with a neurological unit for further testing.

"Lord, Mom's had an MRI, a CT scan, a spinal tap and a biopsy and her results show she has an inoperable brain tumor. My parents are good people and still relatively young. Why is this happening to them?"

In all this time, I never blamed God. I thanked Him. "I'm going to focus on each day's blessings, no matter how small: the sun shining brightly, the last available parking spot or a latte with heart-shaped foam on top. Even though I may not understand it, I know you have a plan God. What do I need to learn?"

There were times when I cried my heart out to God, "Please God, please. Don't take my parents. Please carry us through this, no matter what."

When I found out Mom had cancer I was devastated, "Lord, you promised you'll never leave or forsake us. No matter how difficult or stressful life gets, you'll carry our family through. I know life will come to an end for each of us someday, but you'll take care of us and lead us through it, one step at a time."

Four days after Mom was admitted to hospital, Dad was re-admitted; he was unable to walk and in severe pain. We had no idea what was going on. I left the hospital at 1:00 a.m. the next morning and drove home sobbing. I cried out to God, "Lord, please not now. Please let him live." I'll never forget that moment – I know God heard me; I know because each time I think about it, I feel like crying.

The following morning dad was diagnosed with *Guillain-Barre Syndrome*, a disease that causes the body to attack its own immune system resulting in total paralysis. Even though Dad received immediate treatment, he had to spend six weeks recovering in rehab, relearning how to walk and move other parts of his body. When Mom and Dad were well enough, they were released from hospital and returned home.

August 2015 – It's a sunny morning and I'm driving to visit with Mom and Dad. I think back to the summer of 2013, all that they went through and how life changed for our family. I'm instantly grateful.

"Thank you Lord for letting Dad be cancer free. Please keep watching over Mom. Help her with the cancer and effects of the treatments. I don't know how long Mom and Dad will live, but I'm grateful for the time I get to spend with them. I'll do my best to live my life with purpose and encourage others to do the same with the time they've been given. Lord, I trust in you and I know that you will give me strength for whatever lies ahead."

Lianne Tibben lives on a one acre property in Winchester, Canada, and is happily married with three children. Lianne has been a Chartered Professional Accountant since 1997 and has worked for various high-tech and manufacturing companies. Her specialty is her ability to understand a company's cash flows, its drivers, and how that translates into increased cash and capital.

Lianne has a philanthropic nature and enjoys visiting with the elderly, with the sick, and with whoever needs a listening ear. For many years, she's contributed her skills to various organizations on a volunteer basis. She enjoys writing about life on a personal basis.

Linkedin: www.linkedin.com/pub/lianne-tibben/60/6a3/abb

Skype: lianne.cfo

CHAPTER 18   DVORA ROTENBERG

The Beautiful Light at the End of the Tunnel

The only time I look back is to see how far I have come. I'm not one to talk war stories; I'd rather speak about the light at the end of the tunnel that used to be a freight train coming right at me.

In my opinion, it really doesn't matter whether you're born and raised on a farm, in the projects, or in an upper middle class household with all your monetary needs met; it's still the person inside that experiences life and depending on temperament and upbringing, it determines which path a person follows.

I was born into an upper middle class home. My dad was a physician. We weren't rich, but we were comfortable and didn't want for anything.

From my earliest memories, I remember feeling inadequate and like I didn't fit in.

I never achieved the grades expected of me (no matter how strict my dad was), and if I showed any extreme emotion, my mother would say, "Pull yourself together! Stop crying!"

If the term had existed during my childhood, I likely would have been diagnosed with Attention Deficit Disorder.

When I look back, I always felt like I was standing on the sidelines. There weren't many careers discussed in the circle of friends that my family was loosely a part of. Doctor's kids went to tennis camp, and then onto university to get their nursing, medical, or law degree – none of which appealed to me.

Even though I felt like an outsider, my need to fit in somewhere was very strong.

I started drinking and using drugs at a young age to ease my loneliness, my lack of belonging, and my depression (which I later found out was a chemical imbalance, that can be controlled by medication).

We can always belong to the *in* crowd, IF we do what they're doing. I started university with no self-esteem, no self-confidence and a love for drugs and alcohol, which made me feel like I had both – I was ripe material for a cult.

Fortunately (or unfortunately), the group that managed to get their hooks into me happened to be an extreme form of my own religion.

Feeling like I finally belonged, I went along gladly with their doctrine, teachings and rules. For twenty-four years I lived in their bubble of protection.

Two years into my *belonging*, I was setup on a blind date with a gentleman whom I went out with on seven dates in three weeks. Even though I knew very little about this man, we were married two months later. Sadly, our marriage ended up being an abusive one. Because divorce was frowned upon, leaving wasn't an option.

Then the children started coming.

I was told that if my children came from broken families, they wouldn't find marriage partners in the cult – so I held on. The abuse continued and as it did, my dependency on drugs and alcohol became extreme.

One day, a sudden realization hit me hard – "You're a thirty-four-year-old mom to five kids, and your life is going downhill fast! If you don't do something now, you won't be around for them!"

With a sense of urgency, I began looking for help to deal with my addiction to alcohol and drugs.

Serendipity being what it is, I was accepted into an Alcoholics Anonymous and Narcotics Anonymous recovery program; everything that I learned there stuck.

My life began to improve little-by-little, day-by-day. Another realization came to me when I woke up one morning, "WTF am I doing with my life?!"

I knew I wasn't happy and didn't want the life that I was currently living to be the rest of my life.

On that day, my life did a 180-degree turn.

Even so, it was a long journey. For a while, my light at the end of the tunnel was still a freight train barreling down on me. I had neither a plan for leaving the situation I was in nor any idea how I'd get by on my own with five children. Who would help someone like me?

Shortly after this realization, my ex-husband physically abused me. Waiting around for a plan to fall into place was no longer an option. I HAD to put my foot down now. I kicked him out of the house, had a restraining order issued, and began my long and arduous journey of healing.

I spent two years pulling the pieces of myself together. I found work in a profession I loved and made friends at work and outside the cult. During the time when I was single, an old friend (a man that I had always admired from afar and kept in touch with for many years) asked to date me. I fell in love with him, his city and his country, and we were married.

Life with my new husband was another big turning point for me. People say you have to work hard to make a marriage work. We were blessed because ours was never work—our relationship was easy. We simply accepted each other's wonderful points, ignored the annoying things, and respected and supported each other's path in life.

A few months after we were married, my husband and I had occasion to go to Uganda. I'd never been to a developing country before. It was there that I discovered the endless giving heart of my personality. I came home from that trip a changed person, applied for charitable status and started my own charity. Even though I changed lives and helped save lives, it still felt like it wasn't enough.

One day, I decided to see a friend who specialized in non-predictive hand analysis – something I'd always been interested in and drawn to, but had been deeply discouraged from doing by my religion. This woman knew nothing about me, and yet she shared many truths about who I was, and the challenges I faced. She also revealed that my life's purpose was to give of myself, and to help people dig deeply into the realm of their feelings to discover themselves. That explained why I was drawn to run a charity.

Armed with purpose and information about myself, I now felt the pull and desire to help others find the happiness and satisfaction that I had found in my life. I started helping a young man who said to me, "You can be my life coach."

A light bulb went off in my head. I've always strong intuition, and when I was guided to study to become a certified life coach, I followed it. I also acknowledged and embraced the gift of my intuition by becoming a Reiki Master. This path also lead me to see that I have a special way with people, many more gifts to share, and a warm, giving heart.

After a long, twisted, and winding journey of ups and downs, my self-esteem is strong again, as is my confidence in myself. I know I am blessed.

Eleanor Roosevelt once said, "Happiness is not a goal, but a by-product of a life well-lived. It comes from helping others find happiness."

I do my best to live by those words. Happiness is a discipline. I believe that success is not what we have, but what we have given away. I don't anger easily, don't waste time worrying, and I live each day as it comes, knowing full well that my actions today build on the future I want to create tomorrow.

Dvora Rotenberg lives a happy and joyous life in a new marriage, a new city, and a new country. She has found her calling as a Reiki Practitioner and Spiritual Coach. She lives each day to the fullest and every day brings with it new gifts in order to help others.

Dvora has actively helped those recovering from mental health and addiction issues for more than thirty years. She helps young people trapped in religious communities and women trapped in abusive relationships, where leaving often means giving up, not only a way of life, but also one's entire relationship structure.

Website: www.asprielifecoaching.ca

Facebook: Certified Reiki Practitioner and Spiritual Coach

CHAPTER 19   YARA EL HELOU

My Journey to Finding My Inner Peace

"I was waiting for someone to be my missing puzzle piece, to fit snuggly in beside me and guide me..."

My journey began overseas in the Kingdom of Saudi Arabia where I was born into and raised in a Lebanese family. My mother was my best friend and my father was my mentor – they were my portals for discovering the world. I was the youngest of four siblings and our family unit was very close. My childhood was happy and I strived to make my parents proud. In school, I was a lone wolf. I had no deep connections with my classmates and I was lonely.

At eight years old, my father tells me, "Pack your bags. We are going to Canada." I thought to myself, "Cool! Off to Canada we go. Wait. Where is Canada?" At the airport, I couldn't help but think, "I am finally going to find my place and fit in."

After we moved to Canada, my father continued traveling between Canada and Saudi Arabia, working hard to make money to support our family. I always appreciated his hard work, but there were times when I cried at night, or at school, because I missed him so much. When my father was gone, Adam (my oldest brother) became my father figure; he supported me and helped me with anything I needed.

Adam and I would take long walks together by the lake near our home and he would tell me stories. I felt happy and alive when I was with Adam; he helped me understand the world and feel safe in it.

One day before one of our walks, I thought to myself, the puzzle piece that I had been missing was there all along! It was my brother! He was intriguing, amusing, loving, caring, and kind.

One warm day, while we were walking, Adam started telling me a story that was different from the other tales he'd shared. Instead of talking about fictional characters, Adam talked about himself, that he was a god who was married to a goddess on another plain, and that he was preparing for a battle with his brother. "It's the fight of a lifetime Yara! I can't believe this is happening to me!" he said excitedly.

As Adam continued to share his story, I felt confused. I remember trying to figure out WHY he was telling me this tale. When he ended the story I felt very puzzled.

Four weeks later, Adam took a trip to Lebanon to visit some family members. I missed my brother a lot while he was gone, but beamed inside when my parents announced that he was returning.

When Adam arrived home, something was different about him. Not only was our connection gone, he had no interest in spending time with me. I tried to get him to share with me how the war with his brother went. No luck. As the weeks went on, Adam became increasingly distant. Something wasn't right. I can still see Adam walking in the door with my father after his doctor's appointment – the life and light inside of him were gone; he was an empty shell.

The day I found out that my brother was schizophrenic, my entire world crumbled apart before my eyes and my own inner war started. To fill the huge void left by my brother, I withdrew emotionally and secluded myself.

My downward spiral continued as I started university and had my week of firsts – the first week of university classes, the first time living away from home and my parents, and the first time I almost died. I left the hospital, too ashamed to call any of my family and headed back to campus.

I engaged in a harmful habit typical of many university students. After first year, these habits worsened and began to take their toll on my emotional, mental, and physical well-being. The less I saw and felt of others, the happier I thought I would be. I felt sick and riddled with guilt. I would laugh at times, remembering my brother's stories; I was following in his footsteps, down the path of what society calls mental illness.

After countless sleepless nights, I saw a doctor. I left that office with a prescription for sleeping pills AND a referral to see a psychiatrist for both an anxiety and a Major Depressive Disorder. I was unhappy. Addiction was my escape from people who couldn't understand me. After continuously struggling with my decisions, I wanted to end it all – no more feelings of shame for becoming an addict, or disappointing my parents and family. No more pain at not having my brother.

The mix and match of colorful pills that I swallowed that night went down smoothly. As I lay in bed, I closed my eyes, knowing that when the morning light arrived, I too would be an empty shell.

Morning arrived and my eyes opened. My lips moved, and my fingers twitched – but my legs would not move! I looked at my legs and concentrated on letting the message flow from my brain to my lifeless limbs. They refused to budge. I cried and I hated myself even more. Not only was I still alive, I had paralyzed myself!

I cried to the point where my tears burned my face, and screamed "God help me! Help me please!" over and over. Suddenly, I felt my legs release. Astounded, I stood up quickly, hoping that my brain had fumbled. My legs buckled and I fell to my knees. Again, I screamed, "God help me! Help me please!" trying to concentrate and pray. I bowed my head, closed my eyes, waiting for the sensation in my legs to return. As I felt the blood rush into my legs, I opened my eyes. In that moment, I found comfort in prayer.

That day, I walked for hours, thinking of ways I could repay God for the second chance I'd been given. I found myself and regained the will to live. It felt like I was living a new life. I immediately stopped all addictive behaviors that harmed my body, mind, and soul.

Two years later, I married the man of my dreams, who, through his comfort and support, led me one step closer to the person I wanted to be.

Soon after marriage I started doubting myself, feeling guilty about my past and feeling responsible for the sadness my husband felt about what I had endured. Anxiety attacks and depression followed. Life was dim and dull. I wanted my inner demons gone. I prayed to experience the same feelings I had on my transformation day.

I sought out a life coach to help me manage the depths of my emotions, learned to trust myself again, and began using tools like visualization (which my vivid imagination instantly gravitated to).

I imagined myself strolling by a lake. I sat down on a bench and embraced the silence. The presence of a beautiful girl floating effortlessly came into my mind. Her face was covered by her long flowing white hair and her dress trailed far behind her. Her hair wrapped around me and hugged me gently as she encircled me with bright white light. As I wiped the tears off my face, I embraced the feelings that surrounded me; peace and forgiveness were instilled in my heart.

In that moment, I forgave myself for everything that I had done. I realized that I – not my brother – was my missing puzzle piece. I'd suppressed my personality, values, and who I was to become like him. I began moving on with my life and doing the great things that I'm meant to do. I found and love who I have become.

To encourage myself and keep being positive:

I LEARNed to change my inner dialogue to a happier and kinder tone, instead of telling myself I am failure (which limits my chances of becoming successful), I treat myself the way I treat other human beings: with dignity, kindness, and respect. I deserve no less.

I LOVE myself no matter what I'm going through in life. Each and every decision leads to a self-realization of how capable and how strong I am.

I BECOME a part of the world I live in; I don't just exist in it. As an individual, I have many gifts to help me discover why I'm on this Earth.

FINDing my way through the storm isn't a linear process, it involves ups and downs. Discovering my life purpose can happen at any stage, or age. A hiccup along the way does not mean I've lost who I am; it's a sign of progress, and learning how to overcome obstacles.

BELIEVE in myself and my own strength; both lead me to my ultimate happiness and provide me with a Piece Of Peace.

"...until the day when I realized that my missing puzzle piece was me — my Piece Of Peace."

Yara El Helou discovered her love for the Arts at a very young age, however, it wasn`t until her early adult years that she realized the healing impact it had on her well-being. Having gone through periods of anxiety and depression, spiritual and emotional healing came in the form of writing music and creating choreography. She plays four classical instruments; she also loves to dance, sing, and write. Professionally, Yara works for the Canadian federal government and she is also an entrepreneur. Her business, Piece of Peace, is a reflection of her lifestyle and life purpose.

Website: www.lifeofpop.com

Facebook: Piece of Peace-POP

CHAPTER 20   VANESSA KRICHBAUM

Discovering My Inner Diamond

We arrive on the earth as perfect stardust souls wrapped in bundles of soft, cooing flesh; the embodiment of love, innocence, trust, and beauty. We are adored by our earthy loved ones and nurtured body, mind, and spirit. Somewhere along the way in life, things start to veer away from that perfection and the human experience takes over, imprinting on us the ideas and desires of everyone and everything around us. So it was for me.

The only daughter of a serendipity match, my mother, the young nurse, met my father, the ill German immigrant, in the hospital as one of her patients and nursed him back to health. I was the first granddaughter for both sides and for many years, the only grandchild. Without a doubt, no one was more cherished than I.

For my first eight years, I lived a life where I was cherished by my entire family and most notably, my father. Every little girl is the apple of her Daddy's eye. He gets to be a Prince, without any judgement and be unconditionally loved.

My father being a music aficionado, our home was always filled with classical music, which he whistled to in complete accompaniment. My father had his private pilot's license and took me flying on the weekends in his little four-seater plane. He read stories to me every evening, my head on his belly which I called my "cuddly pillow". I could hear his masculine voice resonating through his chest, filling my mind with tales of princesses, mermaids, and Grimm's Fairy Tales. He instilled fastidious table manners in me and roared like a lion while swatting my elbows any time one landed on the dinner table. Then, as soon as my mother went around the corner to the kitchen, with dirty dishes in hand, he would lick his dinner plate clean, sending me into stifled giggles.

He was my Daddy, movie star handsome, full of adventure, and the Prince of my little girl life. I appropriately put him high up on a pedestal.

But for any person, being put on a pedestal is an unrealistic place to be. People are fallible, learning through their so-called mistakes and life experience, without judgement. My father had his faults, secrets, mistakes, mental health, and addiction issues. He was human. And in February 1974, at the age of eight, I was surprised when I came home from school one day and family was there, visiting with my Mom.

Mom asked me to sit beside her on our sofa, and as she lovingly held me in her arms, she told me that my father had died.

I found out several years later, as a young teenager, that my father's death had been the result of an overdose-induced brain aneurism and most likely, another of his suicide attempts; however, in my young mind I played another story. If I wasn't even good enough for my father to stick around, then likely, I wasn't good enough for anyone.

So then began my internal swirl of inadequacy, worthlessness, and searching. This is where my cracked foundation for future relationships began. I was always looking to others to validate my worthiness. Longing for a connection of mind, body, and spirit that would make me complete and reassure me I was loved.

Fast forward seventeen years...I was in my twenties, being raised by my strong, enterprising mother and my military step-father of infinite patience and calm. I lacked for nothing material, breezed through university and landed in the financial industry where I began my career. All around, my friends were doing the same, interspersed with travel adventures and relationships.

During this time, I met my future husband. The mind connection was instant. We lived in cities two hours apart, but traveled every weekend to be together. Weekday evenings were filled with phone conversations that lasted for hours. There was never any lack of topic to discuss and we did so during car drives, meeting parents, and between sand dunes.

We moved in together after four months of dating and our journey began. We relocated to Ottawa, found new jobs, lived in apartments until we found a house in the burbs, planned a wedding, and had two children. We had it all, with the exception of, my husband's approach to responsibility; with each one added, he withdrew further and further away from me, and with harsh words. I mirrored back to him the rejection I felt. The emptiness and longing, for what the future had promised between the sand dunes, hung over me like a black hole. For two years, we went for couples and individual counseling, until one day, I realized that I had dragged my friend to the altar.

So we amicably separated and co-parented our young children in the same neighborhood.

In between my stay-at-home mom gig, and ramping up to restart my financial career, I started another kind of self-therapy – running. I made time to go to the gym and running became my morning mantra. I carved my body back into what it was in the glory days of my early twenties. This change garnered me a lot of attention and compliments, mistakenly validating for me the thin = beautiful = worthy woman. And so, I exuded this.

My second love relationship is the kind of real life story that I cannot fully write here, for it belongs in a movie like "The Bridges of Madison County" or "Nine and a Half Weeks". This man, whom I had known for years, opened his heart to me and when he did, it unleashed a Goddess of Venus energy that had, until that moment, lay dormant within me. Countless hours in a bubble of passion and love, whisperings of what if, years of longing were fulfilled for us both. Upon reflection, this relationship allowed me to accept and express, the passion that I will always need in my life to be fully who I am.

But our relationship was an affair, and the catalyst that ended his marriage. This relationship came with a hefty price tag: for six years we forged ahead and made a life together amidst a storm of divorces, financial fights, a blended family, right and wrong, shame on you, slut shaming, dead beat dad shaming, how dare you shaming, and I can't do this anymore. We rode the hate-fueled rollercoaster until we were both exhausted. And one day, knowing that someone had to call off the storm...in an act of "if you love something, set it free"...I did.

Here begins my Ruby Red Shoes journey.

As I reflect on my past and think about the wisdom I've learned from all of these experiences, one message from my soul is very clear. I needed to first, unconditionally love myself mind, body, and spirit, before I could have a successful, lasting relationship. My father's departure from this world did not mean he didn't love me, or that I was not worthy. It meant that he did not love himself, or feel that he was worthy.

From my completed marital unions, I finally understand that I can't ask another fallible human being to fill in my emptiness, whatever that may be. It isn't fair to place such a large burden on another person, nor should they expect that of me. Instead, my aim is to bring myself into the relationship as whole as possible. Looking for someone to "complete me" only means that I have more work to do on me.

Any time I get red flags (whether they're about me or someone else) I listen, because they're actually my intuition screaming at me to, "Stop and think!"

I also needed to do my own personal work. To dig through my personal trash can of garbage and throw out any refuse that didn't serve my personal growth.

Instead, I focused on revealing the diamond within me, and started cutting parts away, one side at a time, making tiny cuts until I could see the flawless gem more clearly.

It's been hard work and I certainly didn't do it alone. I'm still in the cutting process...taking my time with it...so that my diamond keeps getting shinier and brighter and it reflects more light.

My diamond is quite extraordinary. It is very strong and it has beautiful color and clarity. In fact, there is no other diamond like mine – or anyone's for that matter – no two diamonds are alike. Each one is unique and with its own brilliance.

The work I'm doing to let my diamond shine is a very worthy way to spend my time and energy.

But honestly, why do I bother?

Because the diamond I'm revealing is my soul...my true essence and the gift I have to share with the world. The world needs more diamonds to shine and share. Interestingly enough, as I step into the light and choose to shine, I'm meeting other diamonds also shining their unique brightness!

Vanessa Krichbaum is a heart centered, holistic, financial advisor. She finds enormous satisfaction is helping her clients align their values and dreams with their finances. As an expert listener, she is able to take the puzzle pieces of your finances and construct them into several projections, thus providing choices for your future.

Vanessa partners carefully with related industry experts, thereby supplying her clients with additional resources, when required. At all times, she is meticulous in the review and maintenance of plans, to ensure the highest good for the client, their family, their business, and the world. Her education is continuous and she is currently pursuing her Certified Financial Planning (CFP) designation.

Email: ovkrichbaum@gmail.com

LinkedIn: www.linkedin.com/in/vanessakrichbaum

PURPOSE

Your Life Purpose is about doing (in your own unique way) what you were brought to this earth to do. Retired, working full-time, entrepreneur, stay-at-home mom - how does it feel when you're tapped into our purpose? How does it feel when you're not?

To experience personal and professional satisfaction on a deep level, we can consciously choose live in line with our Life Purpose. By listening to the calling in our heart and soul, and paying close attention to the successes and challenges we experience in life, we get a sense of whether we're aligned (or not), with our Purpose.

Is the path unusually difficult, or is it easy and deeply satisfying? What happens to us if we detour from the path?

In the stories that follow, ten amazing women share their journey of stepping into and harnessing the power of their Purpose.

CHAPTER 21   EUGENIA RODRIGUEZ

When Spirit Showed Me the Way to My Purpose

In my late twenties, I found myself doing what everyone else was doing: going to work (I was a school teacher), buying a house, getting married, buying nice things for my house...but something about it felt boring. At one point I remember thinking, "There has to be something more to life than this." Looking back, I know now that I was lost, asleep, and unconscious.

Life has an interesting way of getting our attention – to get my attention, my life smacked me across the face three times and said, "Wake up."

My dog, Pacha (who had been with me for twelve years) died, two months later I split up with my husband, and the biggest smack of all (the one that cracked me open) – being told that my big brother had been killed. The pain of it all was so great, that my mind shut down. Back then, I didn't see that these wakeup calls were blessings in disguise.

Eventually, I understood that some things aren't meant to be understood rationally. When it came to my deceased brother, he was a guide on my quest for my true self; his death helped me realize that we are light.

I entered a completely new, yet somehow known, world of the subtle. I realized forgiveness, and that we have an ego; I also realized there was actually something more – that there was a soul, or light that was more permanent; and that it was painful, but more real. This is when I discovered and started practicing yoga.

Excited to learn more, I did my yoga teacher training with teachers who taught from the heart. Gradually, my own heart started to heal (at least on a superficial level) the layers that I knew of and the many layers I didn't know about.

Four years later, just when I thought I had mended the broken pieces, a second round of smacks awaited me (I guess because I was not listening to my inner calling).

As a primary school teacher, I loved teaching, but I started to feel like we were doing something wrong – that we were going against children's nature; we were conditioning them, we were installing ideas we didn't even believe in, we were cutting their wings. I felt a change was necessary, but had no idea how to shift things.

I remember having a very significant dream around that time. I was driving in a red convertible along a windy road in a landscape that looked like the Grand Canyon. My friend, a girl my age, was sitting in the passenger seat.

At some point on the road, instead of taking the curve, I decided to drive off the cliff. I looked at my friend and told her and yelled, "We are doomed!"

She replied, "No, we're not!"

After a few seconds of what seemed like an eternity, we landed perfectly on a completely different road. It was bumpier, but prettier. There were a lot of trees, and animals. The landscape was not arid.

This dream helped me realize that I didn't have the courage to jump off the cliff from my secure job, I needed to be pushed off the cliff. I'll be forever grateful for this insight.

Smack number one - I received the shocking news of my mother's cancer and that she needed treatment.

Smack number two - Going with my mother to her chemotherapy meant that I needed to take some time off from work. The School Director made me choose between taking care of my mom and being a teacher. I was upset with her at the time, but I see now she was sent by the Divine to make me take the very necessary leap I had to take. I chose my mom over the sense of security my teaching job gave me. Surprisingly, the Director saw I was really happy teaching yoga and created a position so that I could teach yoga in the school. It was a savior.

Smack number three - Turns out, being unemployed and having a sick mother undergoing harsh treatment weren't enough of a wake-up call for me. Life with my partner (who I thought was the love of my life), required a lot of effort. Despite that, we decided to start a family. I easily became pregnant and never felt as happy and complete in my life. It didn't last. I lost the baby at six weeks. People underestimate the effect that type of loss has on a woman – unless you've suffered through it yourself. The sadness of losing the baby affected my body, heart, and soul. My partner thought I was being too emotional. I felt misunderstood, my sense of worthiness was running low, and I felt he was very insensitive.

My partner's reaction made me realize that I had been ignoring the fact that our relationship was going down the drain. I was living with the love of my life, but I felt utterly alone.

Despite my fear of being alone, I ended the relationship. With a sick mom, unemployed, heart-broken, and being broke; I drowned myself in self-pity. I learned I was going through what they call the *dark night of the soul* and what it meant. Lessons are best learned when lived, and this experience was a great teacher along the way to show me what I was going through.

As my system of beliefs collapsed, I could no longer make sense of anything. Nothing was real, nothing was valid. I felt stripped away in the darkness of night with unknowing. I had jumped off the cliff, and didn't know if there was another road to land on. I had no control. I tried hanging onto an old belief and memory, only to find out it was not real. My mind could not comprehend what I was going through. I didn't know if everything that was happening was a blessing, or a curse. It was only when I surrendered completely, that I saw the dawn.

My journey isn't over, but now there is a clear path, and I have more trust that whatever unfolds is what is best, and that I have all it takes to make it through any challenge. I know I am here to fulfill a mission, and along with everyone else.

In teaching yoga, I realize this every day. My practice has turned out to be healing to everyone who participates. It has created community and a sense of solidarity. New ideas for projects are being produced. Personally, I realized I wanted to study transpersonal psychology, and am now studying to become a therapist. Many of us in this community have become more empowered and awakened. The beautiful network that emerged has begun to expand.

Everything that happened to me has been a blessing in disguise. I feel like a pendulum that swings with no inner effort. I don't plan anymore; I just surrender to the magic and what it brings along. Life has become very unpredictable. All I know, most of the time, is that everything will be alright, because everything is perfect the way it is.

I'm here to be of service, sharing what I have learned through my experiences; the pain, the joy, the love and hate, the weakness and the strength, the life and death. Sometimes I am standing at the other side of the abyss, to act as a ray of hope for those who are flying across the void, anguished by the darkness. Sometimes it is me who feels suspended in the air, and someone else has the chance to be that light. Teaching yoga is the vehicle I use to get to those places with people, but it also happens in deep conversations, in a warm hug, in understanding our subconscious, writing a chapter for a book called *Ruby Red Shoes* that you are now reading.

The Universe is very creative, beyond the capacity of my own mind. By surrendering to its infinite Love, endless possibilities will arise.

Eugenia Rodriguez was born in Costa Rica and developed a taste for different cultures. She traveled, became a teacher, got married and divorced. Her stable, secure life got shaken by a series of events that opened up a complete unknown path. She is now a yoga/mediation instructor, studying to become a transpersonal therapist.

Traveling is still part of her life and she has two cats. She now walks a path that, even though is a little bit uncertain, is more magical, meaningful, and more exciting. Her life is abundant, in unconventional ways, and she lives in deep gratitude.

Website: www.yogaanantha.wix.com/yoga-anantha

Facebook: Eugenia Rodriguez

CHAPTER 22 SUSAN KERN

Once Upon a Time
I Thought I Had a Dream

There are events in life that seemingly arrive out of nowhere, yet change everything. Sometimes they involve illness, or worse. For me, the event ended up being a Question, "Susan, what is your heart's desire?"

I have looked down from steep cliffs and contemplated what it would be like to fall, into the void; but THIS question pushed me from the cliff into nothingness.

Moments before "The Question", I'd been peacefully living a slightly contented life, being a mom, wife, neighbor, pet owner, and not overly conscious being. It wasn't everything I had ever dreamed of for my life, but I was doing what I was *"supposed" to be doing*, more or less.

I tried to be a good person. (That's good - right?) What may have been missing wasn't really a problem, I told myself, because, "That's just the way it is. We don't always get what we want."

If I doubted that, a popular song's lyrics would periodically remind me of this over the radio waves, "You can't always get what you want"! and I would fall back in line with meeting the needs and expectations of others. Do not mistake me, I loved my life in so many ways and was grateful for all of it. It's just that if you deny what you want long enough, you forget it ever existed. That said, the heart *never* forgets.

"The Question" bounced inside my mind, searching for a place to land, so that I could make some sense of it. I don't know if I realized it at the time, but this was the first time I had really stopped to consider what *I* wanted and what was really important to me, on more than a surface, or material level.

I know that when I was pushed off the edge of the cliff into the abyss of the unknown, a part of me stirred from deep within, longing to be liberated from its prison. In that moment, as I fell helplessly out of my world, the answer to "The Question" was clearly, "I have no idea." I felt the pulsing of a sleeping giant in my chest.

Now, imagine you are living what, from the outside, looks like a perfect life and yet every morning you get dressed to live someone else's life without even being aware of it. It's not a convenient awareness. If I dared to look within, all manner of horrors could be unleashed!

"No. I won't do it. Do you know how many people would be disappointed in you?" I asked myself. That thought was too much to bare, "*Quiet. It's okay. Go back to sleep.*"

And I did—for nearly six years.

"Mommy, Mommy, WAKE-UP!" I felt myself be pulled outward from the space behind my eyes. I saw my daughter, frantic, trying to wake me up. I knew who she was, but very little else. When the paramedic in my kitchen asked me if I knew what day it was, I wondered, "What is a day, and why does this man think I should know which one it was?"

Many tests later I was told that I had, had a seizure, and that they were uncertain what had caused it.

Later in the day I remembered a dream I'd had. I call it a dream; however, it wasn't so much a dream, as an experience: I was standing at a podium. In front of me was a group of Beings. They were very angry. Apparently, I had defied them somehow. I entered into a heated argument with them, all of us yelling at the same time. Finally, I pounded my fist on the podium. They were quiet. I declared, with a power I didn't know I possessed, "**You will no longer control me with fear.**"

The leader of the group looked me in the eye and said, "Fine, be gone with you then." The floor beneath my feet opened up and I fell. I don't know how far I went, but I am sure I traveled through many galaxies, until the point where my daughter woke me up.

There are many levels on which this dream experience can be interpreted and analyzed. For now I want you to imagine the impact of my declaration, "You will no longer control me with fear."

All these years **Fear** had kept me separate from my heart's desire. The connection between the Question and the dream became painfully clear to me – I need to stop putting my head in the sand. Acknowledging these truths ended my life as I had known it. No longer would my heart put up with my inner dialogue of self-denial and defamation based on fear.

Many things changed in the following years. I learned about my fears. I looked at them. Instead of hiding from my fears, I began walking towards them and I took action in spite of them. I learned what it meant to take responsibility for myself and my life. I learned about love when I asked, "What was it that my heart longed for?" The answer was, "Love. My love."

It's such a cliché that "you can't love another, until you love yourself." I'd never really given that cliché much thought, or seen any truth in it; however, when loving myself became my over-riding purpose, I began to acknowledge the strong energies I had been abusing myself with (because of fear), and I started to learn a new way.

Learning an entirely new way of being, was uncomfortable and profound. There were days when I wouldn't get out of bed, because I couldn't face myself. The battle between fear and love raged in my heart and mind.

I read books, meditated, watched movies, journaled, screamed, cried and laughed. I practiced what I had learned and what I preached. As Eckhardt Tolle suggests, *I learned how to make friends with the present moment.*

I made an effort to be aware to *feel* what I was feeling *in the moment*; not just *think* what I was feeling. Many times, the feelings weren't pleasant. I let myself imagine that it was okay to not feel okay. In doing this, I learned to see my self-judgement, and I let myself accept whatever thoughts and emotions came up. I began to *see my Self seeing myself.* Intellectually, I knew I was not my thoughts, or my feelings, but *knowing* this in my mind, wasn't the same as *knowing* it in my heart.

Accepting myself unconditionally, loosened the grip fear had on me. And when I did this, something magical, wondrous and incredible happened—a voice inside me gently whispered, "Susan, I love you."

Suddenly, my prison door was unlocked, and a breeze disturbed the dust on the pathway into the depths of my heart. The tears that flowed in that moment were violent and gentle, joyful and angry. Pent up emotions flooded out, and a cleansing began.

The gentle voice that spoke of loving me – was Me! It was more me than anything I had ever known. Everything in my head that I had believed was true (like what was right or wrong, and good or bad), began to dissolve, layer after layer. Although it felt foreign at first, I gradually learned to surrender to this feeling and trust in my inner knowing.

I tried out my newly discovered ability to observe, accept, and love myself – all of myself – without judgement. I was given access to some very dark and hidden "truths" that I'd believed about myself *(I use quotation marks, because these truths were really choices that no longer applied to me)*.

On one occasion, I was stuck and feeling guilty for how I'd acted in a past situation. I saw my behavior as *not okay* and the resulting guilt had plagued me for a long time.

I sat, breathed deeply, closed my eyes, and imagined meeting my guilt. It took form, and stood in front of me. I looked deeply into its eyes and felt my guilt without fearing it, or trying to run away from it. I embraced the fear, and as I did, I embraced a part of me that I'd separated from long ago. The part of me that hid in fear of my negative judgement was gone. I disowned nothing and I accepted everything. As I let this process unfold, I saw my guilt transform into a brilliant wisp of silver light that swirled toward me and enter into my heart. I was sitting with my eyes closed. A chill moved through my body, my stomach growled and my body twitched. I yawned. Three tears rolled gently from my eyes. A feeling of deep peace and wholeness expanded within me.

The Question "What is your heart's desire?" is years old now. It lives in me each day, as does the gentle whisper of its answer, "To LIVE my heart's desire."

Susan Kern, M.Sc. has been on a conscious path of self-exploration and healing for over eighteen years. Having healed a chronic illness in herself, she guides people with challenging life and/or health situations to trust that they have what it takes to heal, grow, and expand into their true self. Susan sees the obstacles in life as opportunities for growth and transformation.

A scientist, healer, and teacher, Susan nurtures the vision of people living beyond illusion, where they know they are enough, so they can step into loving, accepting, and trusting themselves as the Divine Humans they truly are.

Website: www.susankern.com

Facebook: Susan Kern, Uxbridge

CHAPTER 23   KRISTINE GRAVELLE-RYSTENBIL

My Happiness Barometer is Always Right

As a Scientific Hand Analyst, I'm able to determine what someone's Life Purpose is – including my own and use it to make concrete day-to-day choices that keep me in line with it.

Long before I learned what my Life Purpose was, I was haphazardly living it, by saying, "Yes" to *chance opportunities* that fell into my lap. I didn't have a big picture road map for how all of my experiences, feelings, and talents fit together. I had no idea that by knowing specifically what my Life Purpose was, I would be naturally positioned to attract a great relationship with someone special. I had no idea that by knowing my Life Purpose I would have peace of mind because all of the guess work was gone – I was able to *choose* which activities I needed to do in order to be in line with my Purpose.

On a lonely evening in May 2001, I'm sitting on the floor in my one-bedroom apartment bawling uncontrollably. I'm eight months out of a seven-year relationship and I'm dating again. Unfortunately, the guys who I've been seeing just want to date; they're not interested in anything long term. The saddest part is that I've dated them long enough to have started falling in love with them.

After boyfriend break-up number five, my heart's a wreck.

On that lonely evening in May, even though I'm crying, my heart's in extreme emotional pain, and my mind's in complete static, a realization hits me and I get angry. I look to heavens and say, "I'm done with emotional roller coasters! It's time for me to get my S*#T together so I can meet someone who's a good match!"

"Hey Kris, remember that personal growth course I told you about last month?"

My friend's just phoned me to share that there's an open house on Friday evening, for a course she's taking that weekend. She's calling to invite me out for a couple of hours on Friday night to meet the teacher and listen to what she has to say. "She's a VERY cool lady Kris. She'll be talking about personal growth, breaking patterns, and improving our own lives through working with energy. You and I talk about this stuff all the time. Why not come out and meet her."

After my breakup earlier that week, I think to myself, "You know what? I'm going to that information session! I'm thirty-one, and I'm done getting my heart broken and attracting the wrong kind of guy. It's time for me to figure out what's going on with my psychology so I start attracting great relationships."

On Friday night, I attend the session as planned and love what I hear. I decide that night to register and take the weekend session. Within the first three hours of starting the course on Saturday morning, I know I'm in the right place. I've never been exposed to meditation, intuition, chakras, or energy healing before, but for the first time in my life, my soul's at peace and it feels like I'm doing something that I'm naturally gifted at. When the weekend course is done, I commit to taking a four-year Energy Healing Program with the teacher.

After four years of diligent work, graduation day arrives. I smile as I walk up to my teacher. As she hands me my diploma, she gives me a big hug of congratulations. I am now a Certified Advanced Energy Healer. Yay!

I have always been grateful for taking that program, because it's where I learned how to connect with and have back-and-forth conversations with God and my Higher Self to get the answer to any question I ask.

Interestingly enough, in the final year of my Energy Healing program, I meet a very special man at a single's event and we start dating; it goes exceptionally well. Because energy work and intuition are a fundamental part of who I am, I let the sweet man I'm dating know early on what I'm studying. The main reason I tell him is because, I want to observe whether or not he is able to accept this part of who I am – if he can't, it's a deal breaker.

Even though this man is more traditional in his Christian faith than I, he's balanced in his approach and he doesn't force his beliefs upon me. What I also like is that he's comfortable talking about life and personal growth. He asks existential questions and he's always learning something new so he can grow personally. What a relief! Many of the guys I've dated before had no interest in talking about this stuff; they were happy living their lives unconsciously.

From my previous dating experiences, I know what my tendencies are. I decide this time 'round, to adopt a different strategy. I'm going to use my newly established Higher Self connection to help me pace myself and I'll ask for confirmation on items like when I return his calls and what topics I talk about with him. I find that using my intuition in a dating situation works amazingly well; I'm at peace and I feel grounded the entire time. At one point I even get insight that this man is the person I'm going to marry. Even so, I adopt a "wait and see" approach and I keep on dating him.

The sweet man and I keep on having great dating experiences, which soon lead into something long term. One month turns into seven, and by the eighth month he proposes. Twelve months later, the sweet man and I get married.

In my mid-forty's I realized that I am a woman who thrives in an emotionally affectionate and expressive relationship with a man. I love my husband and who he is; from day one he's has been consistent, constant and openly appreciative. He's never played games with me, or made me question his intentions. I've never needed to ask whether he loved me, felt insecure, fearful, or put through an emotional wringer – he's always been forthright with me about his feelings. From the get-go my husband's been emotionally tender, thoughtful, and considerate.

To this day I continue to use my intuition in my relationship with my husband; its guidance has never steered me wrong.

It's September 2011. For the past twelve months, I've been keeping myself inspired and busy with setting up a small business. To help shift my mindset from working for someone to being an entrepreneur, I enrolled in an online Business Coaching program. After nine months in the course, I'm confused and frustrated – as much as I've tried narrowing down what my business focus is, for some reason I can't figure it out.

One day, I happen to be looking through the online Bonus Material for my Business Coaching program, and I find an audio interview that my mentor did six months earlier. In the interview, she talked with a woman who did Scientific Hand Analysis and throughout that interview she thanked the Analyst for providing her with solutions and strategies that made her money in addition to improving her business, and her personal life.

I thought to myself, "I've spent nine months being stuck and frustrated. I'm done! I contact the Scientific Hand Analyst and pay to have my hands analyzed." When I have my analysis done, I'm shocked. In that session, I finally understand why I've been experiencing all of the challenges and negative emotions that I have been since childhood.

For example, My Life Purpose of Spiritual Teacher is the reason why I've always been attracted to and involved with all things spiritual, existential, and personal growth-related! I'm relieved to find out that as a Spiritual Teacher in the World, it's necessary for me to implicitly trust and act upon the insight my intuition gives me. If I don't listen to it, I can experience feelings of depression, disillusionment, isolation, hopelessness, and extreme mental confusion.

My analysis helps me out on such a deep level, that I take the two-year training program and become a certified Scientific Hand Analyst.

At age forty-seven, I think back on the interests and emotional ups and downs I've had in my life up 'till now. There was a reason for everything and each situation was lining me up to do what I'm doing today. I think back to the impeccable timing of when I met my husband (nine months before I graduated from my Energy Healing Program). Because I was doing energy work and using my intuition daily, I attracted an amazing relationship that beautifully honors who I am.

I am designed to help people who are stuck in some part of their life; Scientific Hand Analysis is the way for me to share someone's roadmap with them so they can start solving that problem for themselves. As I do this work in the world, and use my intuition to help me make decisions, opportunities for me to speak publically about hand analysis and opportunities to analyze people's hands happen regularly and frequently. When they do, I make sure I say, "Yes."

When my Life Purpose and Intuition are at the core of my business, relationship, and life, everything around me falls into place. Instead of spending my time haphazardly guessing what my Life Purpose is, I now look at my Life Purpose roadmap and I take specific actions that keep me in line with it.

With an extensive job history and experience (25+ years in the public and private sector) in Human Resources, Administration, Communications, Desktop publishing, fine arts, singing, and the healing arts, Kristine Gravelle-Rystenbil knows what it's like to feel aimless, depressed, and isolated – even if you're blessed with a positive attitude, an amazing life, and a fantastic career.

As the Owner and CEO of KGR Hand Analysis and The Luv Chick, Kristine helps creative, independent women and professionals to identify what their Life Purpose is, and assist them to harness their power and potential in life, relationships, and business.

Website: www.kgr-handanalysis.com
Facebook: Scientific Hand Analyst - Kristine Gravelle-Rystenbil

CHAPTER 24   CANDACE HAWKSHAW

From Corporate to Glowing Goddess

My connection to Mother Earth has always been strong. Growing up on a seventy-five acre farm, I felt called to spend as much time outdoors as possible. Because I didn't have many friends, I found solace and an understanding of myself and the world when I was in nature. I never really felt like I fit into the world as it was; I was different and felt it deeply. Having now claimed my own truths and living my life as the healer and teacher that I am, my connection to Mother Earth leads and guides my work.

I know what it is like to live a disconnected life; disconnected from myself, and therefore from truly engaging in life itself. I took the route that I was conditioned to see as successful. If I had a good paying job and played by the rules, how could I fail to be anything other than happy? Fortunately the lessons, from the earlier corporate life I'd been living, have been a gift. The gift was the discomfort and disconnect I felt as part of the corporate world; it pushed me to ask really important questions about my life: Who am I and how do I move out of society's norm?

I've always felt I was missing something; that something was me. I had been in the role of the daughter, the mother, the sister, the office manager, the wife, the lover, the friend, but who was I *really*?

In the 90's, I moved away from the corporate world to try the entrepreneurial life of healing and teaching. My decision to do this wasn't as accepted as it is now. I was called many things, but a healer wasn't one of them. So I went into survival mode and returned to a corporate employment.

From my own experience I know that it really is possible to move from a stressful life to greater freedom and vivacity; to heal, to truly love and have compassion for all. But that compassion had to begin with myself. I had to stop being so hard on myself, and embrace the truth that I was unhappy pushing a pencil in a cubicle. I was unhappy living the world's version of a successful life and not following my divine purpose.

Being in the corporate world has set rules of office hours, the number of holidays and breaks, and how much money you could make. Those rules started to make me feel oppressed. Guilt would be bestowed upon me whenever I asked for time off, and I felt like I was a caged bird. I used to get caught up in the gossip, but it never really sat right with me. I felt like I couldn't be around that energy any longer. Being a manager of a team made it difficult to create awareness around gossip and how it was poisoning the environment. When we look at someone we should not judge them, because everyone has a story.

I wasn't doing my healing work. I drank to fit in. I gained weight because I was so busy following the norm of working, watching TV, and eating unhealthy foods. Then I received a wake-up call that scared me – I needed major surgery. I HAD to make changes in my life. I looked at myself in the mirror and said, "Who are you?" I could see my light was going out and I was dying inside. I left that job along with an unhealthy relationship I was in at the time, and moved back to my hometown.

Taking the steps to leave the corporate world again was pretty scary – all of the unknowns, hearing the voices in my head saying, "What are you doing? You can't do that? Who do you think you are?"

Some of my family and friends didn't fully understand what I was doing, which contributed to the disbelief. They said hurtful things, didn't believe in me, and felt I would not succeed. I took the faith and trust I had in myself and in my choices and moved out of an environment that wasn't in my highest good on all levels: - spiritually, emotionally, and mentally.

I took a few months off for myself to figure out what I was going to do. I was divinely guided to open my wellness studio 'Soaring Spirit' in Cambridge, Ontario. I became known as the Reiki Master Teacher, and the Healer, whose hugs embrace you with divine love and bring you back for more. "She has non-judgement, patience, compassion, and flexibility with her clients and students."

I closed that studio after two years because I realized I was not in alignment with my purpose. I felt like I was being run by rules again - times of opening and closing and it was a storefront on the Main street of Galt. I was managing more than I was teaching. I was feeling a huge calling to become mobile – that's what I am now, mobile – so I may spread my wisdom, love, light, and to create leaders.

I see my students and clients as a forest, a tribe, a community. From my own experience of not being in alignment with myself, I now have wisdom and tools to empower them to embrace the essence of who they are, and to transform and grow. I create beautiful soil filled with love, light, and my students are my seedlings. I plant these seedlings and assist them in growing into beautiful trees which create amazing, strong forests.

It would be very easy and safe for me to return to the corporate world, knowing I would receive a regular pay cheque. This would be the normal thing to do, but it wouldn't be in an environment I'd be happy in, nor would it be in alignment with the essence of who I am. I would be giving away my power and I would lose myself in the realm of manipulation and control.

I am empathic. This means I can feel, see, and have a knowing of my environment and people around me. When I am not being true to myself, I have a heavy feeling inside – almost a sick confusing feeling. Being in the corporate world was very draining for me, because I felt everyone's negativity. People always saw me as different. Some were intimidated, some were jealous, and some actually just couldn't be around my positive energy. I actually told myself, "It's okay to be who you are. People will like you for who you are; not everyone has to like you."

It took me a long time not to worry about what others thought of me; I was afraid to speak of who I was and what I did. Even standing in front of people was a huge fear of mine. Only recently have I have felt safe to step out and show who I truly am.

My purpose in this lifetime is to teach and to spread love and light. When people heal so does Mother Earth. I hold a sacred space for people to speak their truth. My soul and my whole being lights up when I teach Reiki. This is how I know I am on the right path.

I am calmer, clearer, and I allow those things that would normally bother me to flow through me and I release them with love. When I am in my essence I feel like I can create whatever I wish, that anything is possible and I feel so alive. I hold a lot of my Reiki classes in nature because I really feel to be one with all that is, you must connect with Mother Earth.

It took me a while to really know that I was worthy of being paid for my healings and teachings. These doubts came from beliefs that healing should be free and made me question if my teachings had value.

I love my freedom to come and go as I please. I love being a teacher, empowering my students, friends, and clients, as well being in nature. People forget that they have a birthright to grow and change and take their power back.

They can say, "No" without fear or guilt. I have taken back my power and I will be careful to not give it away again.

It is a gift, an honor, and very humbling to see my students evolve through Reiki and stand in their truth, and to see them walk more confidently, knowing that their authentic self is the only voice that matters. It brings me further into knowing that this is the gift I am charged with sharing, and it brings all of us into greater oneness with each other and Mother Earth. My experiences and training through my lifetime are allowing me to create leaders, to help them to plug into their gifts, to spread their truths, and heal Mother Earth.

Candace Hawkshaw is a Reiki Master, Teacher, Healer, Channel, Goddess, Intuitive, and a sought after guide. She has a strong connection with Mother Earth, and is someone you feel safe with.

Candace spent years in the corporate world, but one day said, "No more!" She started being and living her authentic self and is now creating a life she chooses without following the norm of society. She lives a lifestyle based on the principles of Reiki; they have changed her life.

Candace is known to create forests of people who wish to heal, and who want to spread love and light.

Website: www.soaringspirit.ca

Facebook: Soaring Spirit

CHAPTER 25   MOIRA HUTCHISON

Life Began on the Road
Less Traveled

When I was a little girl, I had a very close and compassionate relationship with what was my understanding of God. To me God was the life force that sighed through the trees on a windy day – I could feel its presence when playing with my goats, or even the chickens. When I felt lonely, or questioned what my life was about, I found comfort in just "talking" to God.

It wasn't as if I had ever received specific information from God in the way I might if you and I were sitting having a conversation, but I did receive guidance and feelings of "all is well," or "this will pass and you will understand," when I felt misunderstood by, or afraid of my father.

Looking back, I can see that as I grew up, I grew away from, and forgot about my wonderful, comforting connection with God. When things fell apart, I would often run away from my deep divine connection.

At one point in my life, I felt disconnected from Source for a lengthy time, before I took steps to return into the embrace of it, or rather, I should say *consciously* into the embrace of it – because truth is, I'd never left it. I just shut myself off from it, or was unconscious of it—thinking that I had to figure things out, where to go, who to be, who to align with and whom to avoid.

In my early teens, my parents divorced and my father took custody of myself and my four younger siblings. Many people experience this type of upheaval in their formative years; the additional piece in my story was that we moved from Canada to Scotland. In Canada, my family lived in a remote and rural area. In many ways, I was a blissful "country bumpkin" – moving to the hustle and bustle of Edinburgh was a challenge and culture shock.

As the eldest child in my family, I assumed the adult responsibilities of looking after my younger sisters and of being an emotional support and sounding board for my father. In many respects, I had assumed the role of wife and mother, which gave me very little time or space to consider who I was and, who I was becoming – let alone what I wanted to be when I grew up!

With our new life in Edinburgh, I really wanted to "fit in", make friends, and feel like I belonged. Going to school was a rough experience as there wasn't much about me that could blend in; I was overweight, six feet tall, and wore second hand clothing – unfortunately the teasing and comments from my peers at school added to the pressure. Even though I'd been a grade "A" student in Canada, the school we attended in Scotland did not recognize the grades I had achieved. In fact, my father had to argue with the Head Mistress to allow me and my sister to be placed in the right grade for our ages (she wanted to put us a year behind). Because of this, I had to prove my intelligence in a much more dictatorial schooling system. Within a year, I was placed in the correct level for each subject I was taking.

It wasn't until my late teens that I started to find places where I could connect with and make friends; however, this was because I'd started drinking, going to pubs and night clubs. Alcohol removed my shyness and people seemed to like the outgoing, charming, and fun person I became once I had consumed a few drinks! I did have fun during this chapter of my growing up, but I remember waking up one day on the floor of a friend's flat where we had been partying the entire weekend, I could hear birds singing and when I looked out the window, I saw blue sky and sunshine. I realized that it had been a long time since I'd simply sat outside and enjoyed the sounds, scents, and feeling of nature – my connection to Source was calling! This was the sign I needed. When I left my friend's place that day, I also left the party girl way of life behind.

In high school, I took courses that would help me reach my goal of becoming a nurse. One of the reasons that I become a heavy drinker and party girl was due, in large part, to the fact that I was not allowed to train as a nurse. In Scotland at that time, if you had ever sustained any type of back injury, you were prevented from training as a nurse. I'd truly never considered any other type of calling and suddenly this one was gone. The reasoning makes sense to me now, but at the time I felt disconnected and completely at a loss about my purpose in life.

My father worked from home as a caregiver for the social work department; and when he found out about the derailing of my career plans, he suggested that he would go out and get a job, while I stayed at home and took on the role of homemaker—in his words, because I was so good at it.

His comment motivated me to step into massive action and find a new career path. A big reason why I questioned what my purpose was; because that, on many levels, I felt my purpose was to serve my family. Deep down though, I knew there was something bigger for me, something more connected to my own essence.

I left home and joined an organization that promised to train me to be a healer so I could make a real difference in the world. As you can imagine, for someone who had dreams of being a nurse – this felt like the perfect solution. The down side to this opportunity was that in order to be in the organization, their rules stated that I had to either bring my family into the group, or I had to cut ties with them.

For the first month or so, I was able to maintain a relationship with my family, however, it became increasingly difficult, due to pressure from the organization, and because my family disapproved. I decided to cut ties with my entire family because I felt that this was the beginning of me getting into alignment with my calling as a healer.

I learned a lot from that organization, but broke away from it two years later, because I had started to see and feel more and more red flags about how the organization was run and how its members were treated.

The experience taught me some very valuable lessons, the main one being the importance of taking time for inner reflection and checking in with my connection to Source for guidance.

Something I have come to understand about myself is that when something feels right in the moment, I commit to it one hundred percent and give all of me into that direction or path. In the past, this approach didn't always work for me, but serves me well in life now because I have much more discernment. Of course, that discernment was learned through my experiences and my willingness to step up and help people connect with their own version of Source energy—which also happens to be what my true life purpose is!

I truly believe that life is a giant cosmic jigsaw puzzle and that each one of us is a piece in it, each unique in shape, design and message. Our role in life is to become aware and accepting of our uniqueness and how we fit into the grand scheme of things. Once we have built this awareness, we then decide whether we fit into the cosmic jigsaw puzzle, picture side up, or picture side down. In other words, are you willing to let your true essence shine through, or are you going to play small and keep your light dim?

Each one of us carries within a unique and divine spark. Many people describe this spark as their life purpose, or true calling. Whatever it is for you, it is essential that you find meaning in all that you experience.

When you have a sense of what your life purpose or calling is – it's essential to define and feel what your idea of meaning is. Wandering through life wondering why we are here, and what we are meant to bring to the world, yet not being able to see the signs and signals, can actually be the block that prevents us from seeing where we are supposed to be.

Wouldn't it be great if we could just see and comprehend our own inner blueprint? Truth be told, I believe we can access that inner blueprint – we haven't been given an instruction manual on how to do it, but with a little patience and out-of-the-box thinking, it is possible.

Moira Hutchison is a Mindfulness Coach, Energy Healer, Tarot Card Reader, Author, and Speaker. Her specialties range from helping people with broad goals such as life planning and personal balance, to specific goals like gaining motivation and overcoming issues such as procrastination, excess stress, and self-sabotage. She has multiple certifications in energy psychology, hypnotherapy, personal growth, spirituality, and self-empowerment.

Using her own approach – "The Letting Go Process" – she helps people shift from feeling stuck and overwhelmed to being in alignment with their life purpose – inspired, empowered, and actually in control of their lives.

Website: www.WellnessWithMoira.com

Facebook: Wellness With Moira

CHAPTER 26   ALICIA MARSHALL

Put on Your Big Girl Underwear

I believe that we are all born into this life with a purpose and if we pay close attention to the events and life experiences that light our souls the most, then we can piece together our divine life purpose.

As a little girl, my favorite activities included swimming, dancing, drawing, painting, attending church, and visiting my grandparents on the weekends. While doing these activities, my soul shone its brightest.

I was six-years-old when I tapped into part of my life purpose.

During the summer of 1985, after grade one, my mom and I were making a scrapbook with all of the best photographs and memories from my school year. Mom loved to take pictures and document all of my milestones. Everything from school plays and recitals, to chicken pox and head lice were captured on film; needless to say, there were a lot of pictures to choose from.

As we were cutting and pasting pictures into the scrapbook, Mom asked me, "What do you want to be when you grow up?"

I told her I was going to be a mom, an artist, and a priest.

My mother loved me dearly and was very proud of me. In that moment, she reminded me that being a priest would likely not be an option, since priests were men and I would grow up to be a woman.

I was only thirteen when Mom died in a house fire. After her death in 1993, my father gave up my sisters and I to foster care, and shortly after that we became crown wards.

When I was in grade eight I was living up to parts of my life purpose. I found out that I had been accepted into the visual arts program at Canterbury High School. Canterbury is a prestigious Art school in Ottawa known for its elaborate audition process and selective candidate requirements. Most kids would have been excited by this great accomplishment, but not me. I was too afraid of not being good enough. Instead, I settled for something more in my comfort zone. I said no to the opportunity and settled for going to a small neighboring high school. My dreams of becoming an artist slowly faded in my hopeless teen years. I felt lost and unmotivated.

When my beautiful daughter was born in 2005, it was the happiest I could ever remember being. For the most part I felt at peace, yet there was a restlessness inside me about finding my life purpose.

I was called to attend Saint Paul University in Ottawa to study Theology. I remember my first year ethics professor, Reverend Wayne Menard, saying to me in front of the entire class, "You think outside of the box and that is a compliment!"

My face went red. I was mortified at being singled out. At the time, I didn't fully understand what the professor meant, and although he intended it as a complement, it didn't feel like one.

I was half way through my Theology undergraduate at Saint Paul's and I wasn't sure what career or master's program I wanted to pursue. After some spiritual and vocational counseling at the University, I learned that I was not passionate about being ordained and that I felt drawn to pursue a career in pastoral care, namely hospice care (perhaps something secular), in the non-profit industry. Interestingly enough, my counselors at the time, commented in unison on how intuitive I was, but that I rarely listened to, or followed my inner guidance. In that moment, I remember wondering how inner guidance was relevant to me finding my life purpose.

I spent the next six years working and volunteering with the elderly in my community.

As life would have it, my passion and career overlapped into my personal life. My maternal grandmother was diagnosed with cancer and immaculate degenerative eye disease. In addition to my studies, work, volunteer work, and personal life, I was suddenly immersed into pastoral care.

Getting to spend the last seven years with my grandma was as amazing as it was difficult, since we didn't always see eye-to-eye. She was clever, sassy, and strong-willed. Some would say I get these traits from her. On the down side, we could both be proud, controlling, and easily angered when we didn't get our way. Thanks to my grandma, I learned a lot about patience, tolerance, strength, and having a sense of humor. Whenever I was struggling or afraid, she would say to me, "Put on your big girl underwear." and I would laugh.

At thirty-two, I was completing my Theology undergraduate, with hopes of doing a masters in Pastoral Theology. I was a newlywed who had built and moved into my dream home in the 'burbs, and we had a second baby on the way. On the outside, my life appeared incredible, yet on the inside, I felt a huge void that I couldn't explain.

My marriage was lonely and full of arguments and I'd lost interest in my studies. *(At the time, I was in denial about being in an abusive relationship; I was afraid my world would fall to pieces. After I left my marriage, I suffered enormous feelings of shame and failure because I had allowed myself to be in a relationship like that).* On top of that, my grandma, who was my rock, was in the hospital dying and in her final days.

As I sat by her bedside in the stale hospital room, I placed her hand on my seven-month pregnant belly. I could sense that my grandmother was afraid to leave me.

I whispered into her ear, "Put on your big girl underwear. I love you and I am going to be okay." Sadly, she died later that evening.

I followed my own advice and left my abusive marriage. A few months later, I was separated. As a single mom of two, I was financially insecure, afraid and uncertain where to begin, or how to rebuild my life; I had no grandma to lean on.

I wrestled with questions like, *Who am I, aside from being a mom and wife? What do I enjoy, aside from cooking and caring for my children?* I couldn't remember what excited me, or what my life purpose was. I was full of sadness, shame, fear, and grief. I was drinking too much and had isolated myself from my friends. I wanted to change my life, but I didn't know where to start.

On the morning of August 2, 2013, after a terrible night of drinking, I woke and heard my grandma's famous words, "Put on your big girl underwear."

And I listened.

It wasn't easy (deciding to overhaul your life never is), but over the next twelve months, I slowly started to change my life one day at a time. As I did, I started remembering parts of my childhood and the things I had taken so much pride and pleasure in as a child: swimming, dancing, and art. I sought counseling to heal my shame. I started exercising regularly to increase my strength and confidence. I took up painting in my spare time to heal and express my repressed creativity. As I did these things, my life started to change in amazing ways. For the first time in my life, I felt soulfully satisfied, deeply nourished, and validated. My life started to make sense.

Today, my life is amazing on the inside and out. I own my own business creating healing energy paintings and working as a Reiki practitioner. I am surrounded by a loving and inspiring support network and I am in a healthy and loving relationship. There are still days when I feel fear and darkness creep in. In those moments, I remember my grandmother and her famous words, and I *put on my big girl underwear* and go for it!

Alicia Marshall is a Canadian Entrepreneur, Theologian, Energy Healer, Artist, and mother of two living in Ottawa, Ontario. From early childhood, Alicia expressed a passion and aptitude for the arts – especially drawing and painting. She's the owner of AliciaArt Incorporated. Alicia is influenced and inspired by a personal and collective religious and spiritual imagination. Her style is a brilliant combination of bold colors and textures and her paintings are infused with Reiki and Healing Violet Flame Energy. She is a certified Theologian and Reiki practitioner.

Website: www.AliciaArt.ca

Facebook: AliciaArt

CHAPTER 27   JANINE L. MOORE

Living My Purpose at Sixty

"The two most important days in your life are the day you were born and the day you find out why." Mark Twain

True confession. I'm an idealist and a seeker of truth and personal development. Some days, I feel like I just "know" things based on my strong intuition. At times that freaks others out, because I'm able to hear things they're not saying.

I have a unique perspective on the world around me and can envision endless possibilities. I'm a non-conformist who is drawn to being a catalyst for change. This does not sit well with the status quo and bureaucrats, and gives you some insight into why I had a rocky road career path. What it doesn't explain is why I didn't get off that road sooner. What was I thinking? It was mainly fear of the unknown.

I have enjoyed almost every job I've had. What I didn't like so much were the policies and procedures manuals. I thought they lacked the flexibility to accommodate the real needs people have. My superiors often told me they were the ones writing the rules and it was my job to follow them. That didn't sit well with me. I changed jobs a lot. Sometimes, I was shown the door. Most times, I let myself out.

Two years ago, I transitioned into self-employment! What was it that finally convinced me I had to live and work on my own terms?

My journey into entrepreneurship came about after several conversations with a long-time friend. She would ruminate about her job, the boredom she experienced and the long hours she was forced to work. She wanted to quit and work at something she loved, but she was worried she hadn't saved up enough money for retirement. So, she stayed. Less than two years after a long conversation my friend and I had about this, she died. She was only fifty-two.

A quote from Henry David Thoreau has haunted me for many years: *"Most men lead lives of quiet desperation and go to the grave with their song still inside them."*

The older I became, the more I wanted to sing my song out loud and have power and control over my own life. My friend's death is what finally made me take the steps I needed to take to walk through my fears.

I was almost sixty by the time I realized I'd been searching for my "dream job" in all the wrong places. I'd been frantically looking at Job Boards for my perfect fit and sought external validation for my work. I finally realized that my "dream job" was an "inside job" and that the only person who needed to give me permission to express my authentic self was me!

My transition from employee to entrepreneur began with writing a book. In many ways, the book wrote me. *Work On Your Own Terms* was not the book I intended to write, but as the words spilled out onto the page, it became a spiritual journey that made me dig deep into who I am and what I stand for. It made me realize I need to take my soul to work; I could no longer leave it behind during a nine to five workday.

Choosing the path of an entrepreneur forced me to publicly declare my need to make a meaningful difference with my work. I longed for the freedom to use my creativity, and to allow my work to match client needs – not the needs of a bureaucracy. Self-employment became the best vehicle for me to achieve this.

For the past two decades as a Career Counselor, I've helped people uncover their inborn gifts and loved every minute of it. The problem was trying to help people find a job where their gifts could be fully utilized.

I've helped write hundreds of resumes and cover letters. Unfortunately, they often disappeared into a black hole, or the jobs they led to ended in disappointment. It was a disempowering process for me and my clients. I often felt like I was teaching people the skills to go out begging for jobs. I've witnessed far too many people in despair about both their job search or and the jobs they ended up with.

When media reports continue to show seventy percent of people dislike their job, it's a signal that change is needed. I've always thought self-knowledge should come first. I wasn't able to fully express myself and truly utilize my inborn gifts within a corporate environment. I know this is what leads others to choose self-employment. I kept trying to fix a broken system from within a bureaucracy. It was futile.

When my government-funded contract ended, it gave me the time and space I needed to discover who I was and how to express it. Our society discourages this. I knew midlife was a good time to stop and listen to what my heart and soul were seeking. I felt it was something I'd been born to express. I had to find a way to silence my inner critic long enough to listen to my inner spirit.

I'd briefly flirted with the path of self-employment once before; however, I soon jumped back into a full-time job. Being out there on my own seemed too risky. When my employment contract changed to a degree I felt greatly restricted how I was able to help clients, I knew I needed to give entrepreneurship another chance. It was now or never.

Self-employment has challenged me and tested my limits. I discovered it is full of snakes and ladders. I have tripped, fallen down, and been humbled many times. I've also grown in ways I never imagined. It took me decades to learn that my best growth and learning comes from the painful challenges I face. It doesn't make the lessons any easier to learn.

When I am working, I often lose track of time. I am so engaged in the process that I would do my work for free. I can tell you from experience, I put in many hours of free labor before I made a dollar. The fact that I was able to stay with my work during this period, confirmed I had found my passion.

I wish I'd been allowed to work part-time in my field while growing my business, but that wasn't possible. I warn others that sometimes we need another source of income in order to do our "real" work. Following your passion won't always pay the bills. It doesn't mean you shouldn't pursue it. I strongly believe we all have inborn gifts that need expression.

Many Boomer women have discovered self-employment is the best way to express their gifts and enjoy their work. Others have been able to customize a job for themselves in someone else's small business.

I often wonder whether challenges are in our life to test us, and feel that an issue that makes us angry can lead us to our passion. I decided to be the solution to what irked me.

My annoyance at the bureaucratic system I previously worked under fueled the passion for my current work. I felt I was being forced to get people into a job, regardless of whether or not they truly enjoyed it. My wake-up call came one day when I met with several clients back-to-back who all asked: "What should I be when I grow up?" They all expected to find the answer on our Job Board. I knew I had to find a better way to help. I realized I had used a process to help me with my own mind shift.

I call it my **DREAM** ™ formula:

D = Desire – be clear about what you want.

R = Reduce your expenses in the short-term.

E = Engage your intuition, creativity, and intention.

A = Awareness of your core values is essential.

M = Meaningful work is your focus.

Much like the story of the little fish swimming in the ocean while looking for it, my path was right in front of me, but I couldn't see it. My purpose first emerged as a feeling or a nudge towards work that gave me joy. I stopped thinking so much and followed my heart. Once I removed all the "shoulds" from my life, it was my passion and purpose that remained.

I'm sometimes beckoned off-path by the bright lights and shiny objects of consumerism, or crazy promises of fame and fortune. I can't be distracted by that nonsense. Our planet needs more from me.

If you've been harboring a secret dream, now is the time to act on it – because one day it will be too late!

Janine L. Moore (Jan) is a Lifestyle Career Coach. She offers unconventional career counseling to help you discover your ideal work that's a perfect fit for the life you want to live. Author of *Work on Your Own Terms: In Midlife & Beyond*, Jan uses her 20+ years' experience as a career counselor to help women exchange the nine to five job grind for something better. She can help you find flexible work that allows more time for family, friends, and travel.

Contact Jan for a cost-free 30-minute chat to see if she can help you. No strings attached.

Website: www.WorkOnYourOwnTerms.com

Email: Jan@WorkOnYourOwnTerms.com

CHAPTER 28   JENNIFER GEIGEL

My Purpose Through Emilie's Journey

It was the most crying I had ever done. I would fall asleep crying, wake up crying, and find myself crying at random moments throughout the day. I'm not sure if it was sadness, frustration, or self-pity causing all this pain. I kept thinking of my little girl and what she could have been. I had always wanted a daughter; a daughter I could dress up and play princess with; a daughter to chat with and go to the mall. Although I had a daughter, instead of enjoying all the activities I had imagined doing with her, I was walking on eggshells avoiding tantrums, cleaning messes and feeling deeply frustrated that I hadn't gotten the daughter I wanted.

All aspects of my life were affected; my family was stressed, work suffered, and my love life was almost non-existent. I had stopped painting and writing mostly because the creative juices has stopped flowing altogether. My passionate self disappeared; I didn't know who I was anymore and life itself became surreal. I was but a mere spectator of all the events going on around me, unable to move, incapable of making a difference. Autism had invaded my thoughts and stolen my life. I had two choices; continue in this direction and lose myself even more or make an effort to step out of the darkness.

I'll never forget the day I lifted the dark veil that had shielded me from all the pain and opened my eyes. I made a conscious decision to stop crying but my inspiration wasn't my own happiness, or even survival; it was Emilie! I had no time to continue feeling sorry for myself or for my family. I chose to stop listening to the well-meaning people who opted to pity me, pity my husband, my son, and Emilie. I saw that listening to them served no purpose other than to delay my daughter's development even more.

Shutting out the negative feelings, especially the unhelpful feelings of others, I decided to get informed instead. The more I learned, the less I was afraid of autism. There were books and videos describing different interventions and alternative communication systems. I attended conferences and courses, using every free moment of my day to learn and apply my knowledge to my daughter's everyday life.

It was a very frustrating and difficult time; I was exhausted. Sometime it felt as if months of therapy did nothing at all. I remember analyzing the contents of a binder that included lists and lists of objectives for special needs children. The list was organized from easiest to most difficult and all I could think was that Emilie couldn't even do the most basic tasks in the whole binder.

I remember looking at my coach and exclaiming, "This is a list of things my daughter will never do!"

It felt like I was rowing a boat with all my energy, but staying still in thick, muddy water. It was as if my daughter was now stuck behind her own veil, which made her partially deaf and blind to the outside world. She could only see and hear what was right in front of her eyes – what she had chosen to pay attention to. Although she was physically present, she couldn't hear us, see us, or understand us and my fear of her never succeeding made it worse.

My most exhausted and defeated point is when it happened. I was working on an objective with Emilie called Object to Object Association. The desired outcome of this objective was for Emilie to find two identical objects and put them together. There were two rubber ducks and two cubes. We'd tried it over and over again. No matter what I did, she didn't understand that ducks needed to be paired with ducks and cubes paired with cubed. She would cry and throw herself on the floor, not wanting any interaction at all, never mind following a simple instruction.

One day, while practicing this skill something wonderful happened. After I tried the task with her, hand-on-hand, she looked at the objects on the table, matched two pictures together and placed them in my hand! She understood, or at least, she was able to replicate what I had been doing for days and days before.

I was so happy I screamed! From that moment on it was as though her veil had lifted; she could see what I was doing and imitated it perfectly.

It was at that very moment I realized fear was the evil power setting me back.

The more I feared Emilie's lack of progress, the longer it took her to learn. The next few months proved phenomenal with the strength that was given to me through Emilie's success. Not only was Emilie showing progress in many areas including communication, behavior, and social skills, my own confidence and knowledge of the autism world developed into something I hadn't anticipated; the feeling of accomplishment and enlightenment that can only come from helping others discover their potential. I had found my calling, my life purpose, something that I truly love - helping people in similar situations find the inspiration they need to continue. It was amazing!

Realizing that I could make a difference not only in my daughter's life, but in the lives of other children, I started a small business called Connecting Pieces, to help families in similar situations.

Now, not only am I the mother of a special needs child, I am the owner of a unique business in a small community. My objective is to help families with special needs children - especially autism - find the services they require to help their children grow and develop their potential.

Through my work I encourage families to set their fears aside and see that there is hope for the future.

Through sharing my experiences of teaching Emilie, I share my life with my clients. With every new family I meet, I feel a sense of accomplishment. I've hired therapists to help my clients reach their goals, and tutors to help children with academic needs feel more confident at school. I am the person who is making it all come together and I am proud! Parents are thankful for the services I provide, children are improving many aspects of their development and for the first time in ages, and I feel as if I'm living. For me it's like I'm helping the world a little bit at a time. What a purposeful life it is! The pieces of my world have come together.

Now, the next part of my journey is starting. In discovering my life purpose, I have also learned to take time with my husband and watch a movie on Saturday nights - even if it's only on our couch at home. I have promised myself to call my mother often and have special outings alone with her. I take the time to visit with my brothers and chat with my friends. I take turns doing special activities with my son and daughter separately so I can really get to know them as individuals without the competition for my attention or the guilt of having to give all my energy to Emilie. I now work at a school closer to my home teaching a class of eight delightful students with autism. I take the time to understand my students and become part of their lives. I go back to my roots and allow myself time to write and to create works of art. I allow myself this time as it's important to me and important to everyone around me. It is who I am.

Fully immersed in Emilie's path, I had forgotten my own. But the opposite is also true; because of my deep involvement in my daughter's well-being, I found my place in this world as the helper of many. What I needed to rediscover was everything else that I was.

I set aside years of my life focusing on the needs of others. Living and breathing special needs is one thing, but I am also a teacher, wife, daughter, sister, friend, and a mother to two wonderful children. I am also a strong woman who will fight wholeheartedly for any cause I believe in. Connecting Pieces is now part of a non-profit organization that continues to grow.

And Emilie?

She is talking amazingly well, learning to play the piano, and following the same school curriculum as her peers. I'm very proud of who she's growing up to be. Most of all I'm proud of myself for becoming who I am because of my fearless perseverance and dedication to bringing light into the lives of special needs children just like my Emilie.

Jennifer Geigel is the Founder of Connecting Pieces, a service for special needs children in her community. Jennifer graduated from the Department of Visual Arts, then the Faculty of Education of the University of Ottawa. In 1999 Jennifer became a teacher.

She married David Clermont in July of that same year. Jennifer and David live in the small town of Embrun, Ontario with their two children Jakob and Emilie. Their lives were shaken when Emilie was diagnosed with autism at twenty-months-old. You can read all about their ups and downs in Jennifer's Face book blog.

Facebook: Emilie and the Autism Journey

Email: jengeigel@gmail.com

CHAPTER 29   JENNIFER ROSE WATSON

How I Stepped into My Own Power and Found My Life's Purpose

The countdown is on! Six more days and I begin my twenty-one day Spiritual Journey through the mountainous jungle of Peru. This trip is a dream come true for me – I have butterflies of excitement in my stomach just thinking about it.

As the owner of a Holistic Healing Centre and Day Spa, I'm living proof that by dedicating yourself to a goal and your purpose, you can manifest your dreams and achieve anything. I am truly blessed to be surrounded by truly amazing people to share this experience with.

At the same time my life is heading in an exciting direction and I'm in a great place spiritually. It wasn't always like this. In my twenties, I was as far away from my path and living my life's purpose as one could be.

At the age of thirty, I was an observer in my life. I'd sit back and day dream about what I wanted in life and who I'd become. I filled my life with distraction and illusions; I was so skilled at pretending I had another life, that I actually manifested one for myself. To others I appeared happy, but inside I felt like I was dying.

Depressed, overweight, unhappily married, and suicidal, I mentally struggled with addiction and the impact of the different forms of abuse I'd experienced throughout my life. Because of how I felt about everyone and myself, I had become estranged from my children and family. Physically present, yet emotionally vacant, and overpowered by my own failing body and the unbearable weight I carried in my soul – a black hole of emptiness and death. I was drained – mentally, emotionally, physically, and spiritually. I had no desire to live. At the time, my children were the only things grounding me to this Earth; sadly, there were days when even their presence wasn't enough.

So deeply rooted were my issues and damaged was my spirit, that my body manifested illness inside me. Every four months (for no apparent reason), my body would completely shut down. Either I was frequently sick, or in so much pain that I would be bedridden for days, sometimes weeks. In less than three years, I'd undergone multiple operations for reproductive, stomach, bowel and back problems.

Seeing the light from where I stood, was impossible and yet, THERE WAS a guiding light inside me that had always been there, pushing me to keep going. I had no idea what it was, or where it came from. The only thing I knew was that it was the driving force that safely lead me through each and every obstacle and challenge in my life. Even when I felt I couldn't go on, the light inside pulled me through.

My big wake-up call happened in 2011 – on the night I was taken to hospital by ambulance. Scared, because I'd started experiencing severe chest pains, I called 9-1-1. As I waited for paramedics to arrive, with each and every breath I took, the pain worsened and my heart squeezed tighter and tighter – until the point where I could no longer breathe.

As the darkness closed in around me, I remember wondering if I was actually dying, or just passing out. In the moments before I went unconscious, a question came into my mind, "Do you want to live or die?" it asked.

A voice inside of me immediately answered, *"I want to live."*

When paramedics arrived, they found me lying unconscious on my kitchen floor and immediately rushed me to hospital.

I spent the next two weeks confined to a hospital bed because I couldn't stand; each time I tried, the chest pain was so bad it would cause me to pass out. To top that off, because my back and health issues had become too extreme, I was told that I would need to give up my nursing career.

Devastated and defeated by the news about my career and the state of my body, I felt overwhelmed. I lay in my hospital bed wallowing in my own self-pity, letting myself believe that this hopeless situation was my lot in life.

Three days into my self-loathing, the light of my spirit came alive, I got angry and I started to cry.

"I REFUSE to accept that THIS is my life!" I said to myself, "MY BODY, MY RULES!"

That night I surrendered to myself. I prayed and began the process of deeply accepting who I was and taking responsibility for me; as I did, my body began to resonate with love and a knowing that I'd found my truth.

As mysteriously as it appeared, within one week of making this shift, the pain in my heart disappeared. My doctors never did figure out what caused my heart condition; at the time what mattered to me most was that the pain was gone and I had my life back.

As I released the emotion, pain, and suffering that I'd been holding onto for years, I stopped wearing the victim badge and making excuses for everything that had happened to me. I began surrounding myself with people who saw the best in me and gave me opportunities to shine. I quit living in fear and self-judgment and started to forgive myself (and others) for their wrong doings. I also started paying attention to the characteristics in others that I didn't like; these people were reflecting back a part of me and giving me an opportunity to learn about it more fully.

As I adopted holistic approach to healing my life, I went on a journey to learn about Reiki, Crystal Healing, and meditation. Everything that I learned felt perfect and right. As the next step in my spiritual evolution, I became a certified practitioner in each these areas. From there I went on to study Chakra Balancing and yoga and I'm now studying Shamanism.

In the years following my heart shift, I watched my life transform in astounding ways that let me heal my mind, body, and soul and have the life I wanted. Through each of my challenges and the personal growth that came from it, I realized that my life's purpose was to help others heal. My experience was so transformative that I decided to share my knowledge with the world, and teach people to heal themselves.

My two-week stay in hospital began the journey to some of my most profound awareness's:

- Breathe. To be present in every moment, I learned how to breathe, sit in my own energy and listen for the answers I seek. We come into this world with a breath and we leave this world with a breath – we can control everything in life with our breath.

- My past doesn't define me. We only get one chance at this life to make every moment count. If a situation does not serve me, or my highest good, I release it so something new can enter my life to help me find peace and balance.

- There are times when I can't control what happens to me; however, what I do have control over is what happens next and how I allow a situation to affect me.

- A life that challenges me, changes me. Challenges force me to grow. In my life, I chose to rise above the pain, disappointment, and resentment that I was carrying around when I was hurt. I chose to NEVER give up, no matter how uncomfortable life made me feel.

- Forgiveness was the special gift I gave to myself; it let me move forward and grow from my experiences with no self-judgement...only self-love and a purpose.

I still remember that day in the hospital and how it felt to take back my power, and begin creating the life I wanted. I was forced to ask myself, "Jennifer, what makes you happy?" I set my dreams high, and went out to get it. This brought me to places I'd never imagined I be in.

The young woman who used to wait and yearn to become who she wanted to be, has since blossomed into a beautiful spiritual being who realized that she had the power all along!

As soon as I chose to Own my Power and find my Life's Purpose, my heart and soul shone so brightly, there was never reason to look back. I now look FORWARD and create new adventures for what lies ahead!

Jennifer Rose Watson is a Spiritual Teacher, Energy Worker, Certified Crystal Healer (C.C.H.), Reiki Master/Teacher, Clairvoyant, Author, and Speaker. Her specialties are working with people to create personal healing within so they are able to move forward on their life's path.

Jennifer's constant pursuit of the Healing Arts reflects deeply on her love for nature and humanity. Her fascination with balancing the body's intuitive energies along with the physical and emotional states of the body is transformational to witness. Her work is truly unique, as her journey and wisdom are led by her connection to her higher consciousness and her connection to source energy and God.

Website: www.trueessencehealing.ca

Facebook: True Essence Healing Centre

CHAPTER 30   ELIZABETH MORELLE

How Creativity Rocked My World

By the time she was two-years-old, she felt utterly unlovable. Even her teddy bear's cold glass eyes stared at her defiantly and confirmed it. They tied her down to a bed in the Great Ormond Street Hospital, whilst they "examined" her, keeping her there (at the age of eighteen months) away from her mother and father for an entire week.

She did not thrive. She was a "sickly child." Her grandfather had died six weeks before she came into the world. She was born into an atmosphere of grief and mourning, in sixties' Britain, to a beautiful and glamourous, yet vain mother, who now had three children under the age of five. It was an era where children were to be seen and not heard; in her home the less a child was seen, the better. Her parents did their best with what they knew and followed the trend of the times: bottle feed infants every four hours, then leave them alone to cry.

Being a sensitive child, her parents had a hard time understanding her. When she came racing home with a bunch of dried seed heads, she was excited to show them the outrageous geometric shapes and the tiny seeds rattling inside. All they could see was a bunch of ugly, dead weeds.

"Why can't she pick pretty flowers like other little girls do?" they asked. This little girl was different.

"Look at your rat's tails!" her mother would shout, angrily scraping the hair brush down, pulling harshly through the tangles of windswept hair, until the young girl scrunched up her face in pain.

At school she was "too small," although appreciated; at home she was too talkative, a nuisance.

"Oh shut up Elizabeth! " her father screamed at her one evening at the supper table – and she promptly did. Silent now, she slunk around the house, and learned to be invisible: to avoid the tyranny of her father, the brunt of her eldest brother's meanness, and her mother's unending criticisms and put-downs.

Daily, she felt her mother striving to force her to be someone else, something better, something different from who she was. She did not fit and had no one to turn to. At night, lonely and frightened, she cried herself to sleep. Fear, anxiety, and depression followed her into her teens and early adulthood. Not having learned how to be in the world, she felt as small as a mouse and as worthless as a used candy wrapper. Painfully shy, withdrawn, repressed, and depressed – she felt utterly unlovable, out of place, and hideous. She was the archetypal ugly duckling.

Through her twenties, she struggled, trying to make sense of her world, her depression, and her constant state of grief. Her dream was to be an artist, but according to her father, this would be a very foolish choice, so she made other foolish choices instead.

She entered into a very destructive relationship and marriage that left her severely traumatized both emotionally and psychologically. After fourteen long, miserable years, she left her marriage. Sadly, the perpetrator (her ex-husband) spent the next decade hounding, harassing, and trying to control her with financial and litigation abuse. He even went so far as to pit her own children against her – to make her suffer.

This woman and mother knew about the dark night of the soul, how it felt to be in the depths of despair, and wish that life were over so that she could be released from the pain of her existence. For years, she struggled unsuccessfully to get out of the dark pit of hopelessness.

Time in nature and her search for self-expression were her only solace.

Having grown up "without a voice" she tried for years to "give voice" to that within her which longed to be heard. A gifted healer in Scotland once told her that she had a beautiful singing voice that came through her when she was open to the Divine expression of the universe; however, depression shut her down, and kept the lid on tight. Many years went by. She did not sing, just suffered.

When she tried to sing again, the beautiful voice was gone. Like Parsival and the Holy Grail, she'd lost the priceless treasure; in turn, she spent many years searching for it, to no avail. She would catch occasional glimpses of it, but could never could re-establish, or root the voice in her body-mind as it had been before.

She sang, she danced, she painted. She created. Sometimes she wrote poetry. She experimented and found ways (through song and sound) to tap into her body's wisdom and express what needed to be heard. She caterwauled and wailed; she howled and bawled; she groaned and yawned; she writhed, thrashed and twisted; she lay still.

As she created, she healed. She began to work with others, experimenting and using the voice and movement, language and words to come to a place of openness, freedom, hearted-centered belonging and acceptance. Her voice and soul had the space to be itself.

This Wounded Healer found ways to bring solace, joy, integration, and connection to others through her work. Through her own experimentation, she discovered ways to work with the wounds of trauma and had powerful results when working with others.

After fifteen years of extensively working with the voice, she still hadn't succeeded in finding her own. As the weight of this truth sank in, so did the weight of needing to accept it.

She was reminded of a visualization technique, where she imagined the Divine surrounding her, connecting to her and infusing her voice with infinite Love. In that moment, a miracle happened! In the instant she realized that Divine Love was the key, her voice came forth! As she rested in the presence of the Divine and as she allowed it to move through her, her voice became free and soared through her and beyond her! In that moment, she realized her voice had never been lost, its power had been within her all along!

About this same time she learned of Saraswati, the Hindu goddess of music, melody, muse, speech and language, the arts, creativity, wisdom and learning, who used the healing, purifying power of abundant flowing water. The *flow* of each of these activities brings about the purification of a person's essence.

In Sanskrit, Saraswati can be translated as "one who leads with the essence of self-knowledge". Saraswati is often clothed in white (a symbol of the highest reality), and is seated upon a white lotus representing truth, light, and knowledge. She loves the rhythm of music, and the representation of feelings or emotions expressed in speech or music. Saraswati is the ruler of the throat chakra. Saraswati is often accompanied by a swan, a symbol of spiritual perfection, and a peacock, symbolizing the celebration of dance and the ability to eat poison (snakes) and transform it into beautiful plumage.

Upon hearing of Saraswati, her twenty-five year fascination with the voice, communication, and swans, suddenly made sense. She chose to express her feelings and the energy of her Infinite Self through speech, song, art, movement, and dance. The poison she'd been forced to eat over many years has transformed into the beautiful plumage of her life.

Years ago, she did a painting of a woman dressed in white, before the full moon, accompanied by a swan, a peacock, and a cheetah. She did not know why, only that she had been drawn to do this. She would often use peacock imagery in prints and masks that she made and she felt very connected to swan energy over the years. The long neck of the swan represents the bridge between heart and head, (the throat chakra)!

At one time she lived right on a beach by the ocean and would go down and feed the swans who came there each winter. She loved their graceful ease and beauty! It seems that Saraswati had been guiding her all along, through the darkness and pain and into the Joy, Love, and Gratitude she now experiences daily.

I am here today as a writer, a vocal improviser, a community builder, a lover of life and especially of nature, a poet, artist, and creator. The *"She"* in this story is me, and the story of Saraswati is my own.

We each have themes in our life, and are each on a journey back to ourselves. As women, Divine feminine energy guides our life, calls us to transform into the swan we are meant to be, and to find our calling so we can be of service in the world around us.

In remembering that I have the power within me and that I have it for life, I have stepped into the fullness of my being and become the wonderful swan I longed to be! My journey has been a challenging one, but in standing where I am now, now I feel blessed. In turn, I honor each Sweet Sister that I meet.

Ella (Elizabeth) Morelle is a Registered Clinical Counselor and Women's Coach living on beautiful Vancouver Island, British Columbia. She works with smart and savvy women who are tired of playing small and hiding their light, and who long to find their Soul Song and embrace the passion and power of a life well-lived. Helping other women find their true voice is Ella's passion, her way of being of service in this world, using her creative gifts to help others whilst remaining true to herself and her own need for creativity.

Website: www.elizabethmorelle.com

Facebook: Sacred Hoop Healing: Elizabeth Morelle, MACP, RCC

CONCLUSION

The Ruby Red Shoes journey starts the moment we're born into this world and begin stepping into the blessings and challenges that ultimately align us with our divine calling.

As we have seen in the chapters of this book, the spirit of each woman surfaces at a crucial moment where she chooses to step into mastery in her relationship, her intuition, or her purpose.

Please know that the women in *Ruby Red Shoes* are no different than you; however, through their journeys, they are showing you that it's okay to take the next step to your heart, your self-actualization and your personal power.

Just as this book IS a homecoming for women back to who they really are, no one said the journey would be an easy one. It is inevitable that life will throw challenges your way. Will you continue to walk that challenging road alone, or will you choose to ask for a hand to hold so the journey doesn't feel so dark and lonely? Will you use your Inner Wisdom to help you make decisions? Will you step into your Purpose so you can experience the successes and challenges you were designed to have? What is your story?

Did you resonate with any of the women you've encountered in this book? Please know that your sisters are here to be of service to you – reach out and connect with them through the contact information they have provided.

Were you moved by any of the stories you read? Spread the word and tell other women about *Ruby Red Shoes: Empowering Stories on Relationship, Intuition and Purpose.* By doing so, you connect women with other women who have had similar experiences and allow them to find solace and support.

It is time for us to join hands with women around the globe to create a ripple effect that connects each of us to one another. To know more about the Ruby Red Shoes Sisterhood, please reach out and contact me at info@rubyredshoes.ca.

Please remember that the most valuable resource you have in your life is YOU! May you astound and amaze everyone as you travel on your own Ruby Red Shoes journey.

Love, big hugs and blessings,

Kristine